THE OFFICIAL
Arsenal
SUPPORTERS' BOOK

CHAS NEWKEY-BURDEN

CARLTON
BOOKS

Picture credits

The publishers would like to thank the following sources for their kind permission to reproduce the pictures in this book.

Picture Quiz Photography © **Arsenal Football Club Plc** with the following exceptions:
Colorsport: 6A, 6B, 6C, 6D, 7B, 7D, 8A; /Andrew Cowie: 2A, 3B, 3C, 5B, 7C, 8B, 8C; /Stuart MacFarlane: 1C
Getty Images: /Leonard Burt: 3A; /Evening Standard/Hulton Archive: 1A; /Alexander Hassenstein/Bongarts: 4B; /Scott Heavey: 4A; /Jan Kruger: 4C; /Oli Scarff: 5C; /Charles Temple Dix/Fine Art Photographic: 5D
Press Association Images: /Niall Carson
Rex Features: /Neil Genower: 5A

Every effort has been made to acknowledge correctly and contact the source and/or copyright holder of each picture and Carlton Books Limited apologises for any unintentional errors or omissions that will be corrected in future editions of this book.

Contents

Introduction

As every Gooner knows, Arsenal FC is the greatest Club in the world. Since its formation in 1886, Arsenal has become a name synonymous with footballing class, skill and achievement. The Club has won 13 league titles, 10 FA Cup finals and two major European trophies, and won over millions of fans in the process. In *The Official Arsenal Supporters' Book*, the reader will find everything any fan could want to know about his or her favourite Club.

The book kicks off with a chapter of Arsenal facts and trivia, in which super stats and random factoids are intriguingly combined. Then, you can find profiles of Arsenal's great managers and reviews of Arsenal's championship and cup-winning campaigns, plus potted biographies of a host of Club legends from Cliff Bastin and Cesc Fabregas to Tony Adams and Liam Brady. Classic European nights are also recalled, including the 1994 European Cup-Winners' Cup final win over Parma.

You can also delight in a chapter of Arsenal fantasy teams and a collection of memorable Arsenal quotes. Practise your vocals in our compilation of supporters' songs and chants, before testing your wits in the ultimate Arsenal supporters' quiz.

All in all, this is the perfect read for any dedicated Gooner, which should intrigue, amaze and entertain all fans – much like the team has done on so many mega occasions. Enjoy!

CHAPTER 1

Arsenal Facts & Trivia

Football is a game of opinions, they say – and that is true. Yet it is also a sport of facts, statistics and trivia. In this, the first chapter of the book, you will find a treasure trove of trivia, a fabulous amount of facts and a succession of statistics.

Over the coming pages you can regale yourself with hundreds of fascinating facts and stats about the Gunners. This includes details about the players, the managers, the fans and the stadia that have shaped the history of this fine Club. There are a smattering of "oddball" facts as well as loads of serious statistics. You can read the lot in one sitting, or dip in and out as you fancy.

So if you want to read about famous Gunners fans, find out which players have scored the most hat-tricks for the Club, study Arsenal's European record in full, or find out which player is plagued by a dream about guinea pigs and a horse, you have come to the right place. From Denis Compton to Alex Oxlade-Chamberlain, all Gunners life is here.

So what are you waiting for? Turn the page and tuck into a red-and-white feast. And why not entertain and bamboozle some of your fellow Gooners with the facts you learn in the pages ahead.

The trophy cabinet

League champions (13 times)
1931, 1933, 1934, 1935, 1938, 1948, 1953, 1971, 1989, 1991, 1998, 2002, 2004

FA Cup winners (10 times)
1930, 1936, 1950, 1971, 1979, 1993, 1998, 2002, 2003, 2005

League Cup winners (2 times)
1987, 1993

European Fairs Cup Winners
1970

European Cup-Winners' Cup
1994

First north London derby

Arsenal's first victory over rivals Tottenham Hotspur came on 9 March 1889. The score? One-nil to the Arsenal.

Drake's century rush

Ted Drake took just 108 matches to score 100 goals for the Gunners.

Brotherly love

The most recent instance of two brothers both appearing for the Gunners is that of the Toure siblings: Kolo (who joined in 2002) and Yaya (who had a trial with the Club in 2005). The earliest instance came way back in the nineteenth century, when Robert and George Buist both turned out for the Club.

Arsenal's first Premier League match

v Norwich City (home) – 15 August 1992
Lost 2–4 (Bould, Campbell)

The Emirates eight

The first eight Premier League matches at Emirates Stadium ended either 3–0 or 1–1.

Peculiar injuries

David Seaman: broke a bone while reaching for a television remote control. **Perry Groves**: knocked his head against the roof of the dugout while celebrating a goal. **Charlie George**: cut off one of his fingers in a lawnmower accident.

Low attendance

The lowest home attendance at Highbury was against Leeds United on 5 May 1966, when just 4,554 fans turned up. That's less than 1/10th of today's average gate.

Planet Arsenal

A number of overseas clubs have Arsenal-related names including Canada's "London City Gunners", the curiously entitled "Arsenal Wanderers" of Mauritius and "Arsenal Kiev" of the Ukraine.

Some famous Arsenal fans

Idris Elba	actor
Melvyn Bragg	broadcaster
Nick Hornby	author
Jack Whitehall	comedian
Chris Hollins	broadcaster
Kathy Burke	actress
Matt Lucas	comedian
Dermot O'Leary	broadcaster
Rizzle Kicks	pop band
Roger Daltrey	rock star
Mo Farah	athlete
Tony McCoy	jockey
Ian Poulter	golfer

Middle class

Sol Campbell's middle name is Jeremiah, while Bob Wilson's is Primrose.

American dream

The first Gunner to play in North America was Joe Haverty, who joined the Chicago Spurs in 1967.

Sixteen at the double

The Gunners used just 16 players during the double-winning 1970–71 season.

Getting shirty

The first use of shirt numbers in English football came in an Arsenal v Chelsea clash in August 1928.

One-nil to the Arsenal

The most common scoreline during season 2012–13 was 1–0. It was just like the good old days!

Leading appearance-makers

David O'Leary	722
Tony Adams	669
George Armstrong	621
Lee Dixon	619
Nigel Winterburn	584
David Seaman	564
Pat Rice	528
Peter Storey	501
John Radford	481
Peter Simpson	477

Arsenal win the World Cup!

When France beat Brazil in the 1998 World Cup Final, the *Daily Mirror* ran a front page headline featuring Gunners stars Patrick Vieira and Emmanuel Petit celebrating, with the headline "Arsenal Win the World Cup".

The derbies of David

Arsenal v Spurs was just one of five derby matches played in by David Platt during his illustrious career. The others were:

> **Crewe** v Chester City
> **Aston Villa** v Birmingham
> **Juventus** v Torino
> **Sampdoria** v Genoa

Out of Africa

Kolo Toure is the highest African appearance maker for the Club, having represented Arsenal in 269 matches.

Out of (South) Africa

The first non-European player to represent the Gunners was Dan Le Roux of South Africa, who signed in 1957. The second, John Kosmina of Australia, did not join until 1978. There have been quite a few since.

Leading hat-trick scorers

Jimmy Brain	12
Jack Lambert	12
Ted Drake	11
Ian Wright	11
Thierry Henry	9
Doug Lishman	8
David Herd	7
David Jack	7
John Radford	7
Joe Baker	5
Ronnie Rooke	5

Note: *Doug Lisham and Jimmy Brain both scored hat-tricks in three consecutive games for the Gunners.*

Freedom of the Borough

In October 2004, Arsenal manager Arsène Wenger and Club director Ken Friar were both awarded the Freedom of the Borough of Islington.

An ever-present debut

Season 2012–13 was the debut season of Santi Cazorla. He was the only member of the squad to appear in every Premier League match.

Abide With Me

Since the 1927 FA Cup final between Arsenal and Cardiff City, the first and last verses of Henry Francis Lyte's famous hymn are traditionally sung before the kick-off of the match.

Terrific against Tottenham

Between 19 March 2000 and 31 October 2009 Arsenal went a record 20 consecutive league games unbeaten against Tottenham Hotspur. Arsenal have never gone more than five consecutive league games without beating Tottenham.

Super subs

Arsenal's substitutes scored more goals than those from any other club during the 2009–10 season. Of the 83 league goals struck by the Gunners in that campaign, 15 came from players who started on the bench.

Leading Arsenal goalscorers

Thierry Henry	228
Ian Wright	185
Cliff Bastin	178
John Radford	149
Jimmy Brain	139
Ted Drake	139
Doug Lishman	137
Robin van Persie	132
Joe Hulme	125
David Jack	124
Dennis Bergkamp	120

Good old Leslie!

On 15 November 1950, Leslie Compton made his England debut against Wales – at the ripe old age of 38 years and 64 days. It made him the oldest ever outfield debutant for his country.

Arsenal nicknames

Liam Brady	Chippy
Bob Wilson	Willow
David Seaman	Safe Hands
David Rocastle	Rocky
Malcolm Macdonald	Supermac
David O'Leary	Spider
Nigel Winterburn	Nutty
Theo Walcott	Lewis [Hamilton]
Arsène Wenger	The Professor
Paul Merson	Merse
Dennis Bergkamp	The Iceman
Tomas Rosicky	Little Mozart
George Graham	Stroller
George Armstrong	Geordie
Oleg Luzhny	The Moose
Alan Smith	Smudger

Villa and Villa again

The first and 50th matches at Emirates Stadium were both against Aston Villa – and both ended in 1–1 draws. What a coincidence!

Victoria Concordia Crescit

The Club's latin motto means Victory Through Harmony.

Highest-scoring draw

6–6, vs Leicester City, 21 April 1930.

Doing the laundry

The North Bank at Highbury was originally called the Laundry End. Hence all the clean sheets!

Animal magic

• Two hawks, named Flossie and Rebel, have patrolled Emirates Stadium to scare off pigeons.
• Club legend has it that a horse fell into a hole when Highbury's North Bank was being built in 1913. However, when the stadium was demolished in 2006, only a single horseshoe could be found.
• During a Champions League tie with Villarreal in 2006, a squirrel ran onto the Highbury pitch, disrupting play. It showed considerable speed and nimbleness before it eventually sped off.

Ladies first

The Arsenal Ladies won their first trophy in 1992, grabbing the FA Women's Premier League Cup.

Jens keeps them at bay

Between October 2005 and April 2006, Arsenal went 10 UEFA Champions League games without conceding a goal. The man between the sticks? Jens Lehmann.

Average 20th century league finishes by decade

1900s	17.3
1910s	11.0
1920s	11.8
1930s	3.5
1940s	6.3
1950s	6.1
1960s	9.6
1970s	8.3
1980s	5.3
1990s	4.6

Notable Arsenal captains

Tom Parker	Frank McLintock
Alan Ball	Eddie Kelly
Pat Rice	Graham Rix
David O'Leary	Kenny Sansom
Tony Adams	Patrick Vieira
Thierry Henry	Cesc Fabregas
William Gallas	Robin van Persie

London calling

The first English league game to be broadcast on the radio was Arsenal's 1–1 draw with Sheffield United on 22 January 1927.

Super Swede

Arsenal's leading Scandinavian appearance-maker is Freddie Ljungberg, who made 328 appearances for Arsenal. He's now an ambassador for the Club.

Highbury heroes

Arsène Wenger is the Arsenal manager who won the most league matches at Highbury, with 134 victories. Bertie Mee is in second place with 119 wins.

Herbert Chapman's innovations

- He introduced the semi-circle on the edge of the penalty box.
- He suggested that, at FA Cup finals, both teams emerged from the tunnel side by side.
- He changed the ball colour from brown to white, as the former was harder to spot on muddy pitches.

The first shoot-out

The first penalty shoot-out the Gunners took part in was against Valencia in the 1980 European Cup-Winners' Cup Final. The Spaniards won the shoot-out 5–4, after the game had finished 0–0 after extra time.

Frank's first from fans

The first winner of the official supporters' club player of the year award was Frank McLintock, in 1967. Liam Brady was the first Gunner to win the PFA player of the year award. The Irishman lifted it in 1979.

Set the Sat Nav to CF10

Between 2001 and 2006, Arsenal played in four FA Cup finals and four Community Shields at the Millennium Stadium, Cardiff.

High and low points

The lowest points tally the Gunners have amassed came in the 1912–13 season, when they managed just 18 points. The highest points tally came in 2003–04 when they totalled 90 points.

Double season goalscorers

Thierry Henry	25	2001–02
Ray Kennedy	21	1970–71
Dennis Bergkamp	19	1997–98
John Radford	17	1970–71
Marc Overmars	14	1997–98
Freddie Ljungberg	14	2001–02
George Graham	12	1970–71
Dennis Bergkamp	12	2001–02
Sylvain Wiltord	12	2001–02
Charlie George	10	1970–71
Ian Wright	10	1997–98
Robert Pires	10	2001–02
Ray Parlour	9	1997–98
George Armstrong	7	1970–71
Peter Storey	6	1970–71
Ray Parlour	6	1997–98
Eddie Kelly	5	1970–71
Frank McLintock	5	1970–71
Nwankwo Kanu	5	2001–02

Goal-shy champions

The team that wins the league title is not necessarily the highest scoring side of the season. Arsenal discovered this in the 1937–38 season, when they were crowned champions despite having scored fewer goals than Manchester City – who were relegated that season.

Leading appearance-makers at Highbury

Tony Adams	262
David O'Leary	256
George Armstrong	248
Lee Dixon	220
Nigel Winterburn	215
Bob John	214
David Seaman	202
Pat Rice	199
Eddie Hapgood	197
Peter Storey	190

Two great away days

The Gunners have twice clinched the league title at the home of the defending champions. This happened in 1989, when Arsenal beat Liverpool 2–0 at Anfield, and in 2002, when they beat Manchester United 1–0 at Old Trafford.

Speading the love

In the 2012–13 season, Arsenal were the only side to have four separate goalscorers – Santi Cazorla, Olivier Giroud, Lukas Podolski and Theo Walcott – reach double figures. Arsenal also had the second best defensive record in the Premier League.

Honoured indeed

Denis Compton was the first Arsenal player to receive a civilian honour when he was awarded the CBE in 1958. Subsequent Gunners to be similarly honoured include Billy Wright (CBE), Pat Jennings (MBE and OBE) and David Seaman (MBE).

Arsenal managers

1894 – 1897	**Sam Hollis**
1897 – 1898	**Thomas Brown Mitchell**
1898 – 1899	**George Elcoat**
1899 – 1904	**Harry Bradshaw**
1904 – 1908	**Phil Kelso**
1908 – 1915	**George Morrell**
1919 – 1925	**Leslie Knighton**
1925 – 1934	**Herbert Chapman**
1934 – 1947	**George Allison**
1947 – 1956	**Tom Whittaker**
1956 – 1958	**Jack Crayston**
1958 – 1962	**George Swindin**
1962 – 1966	**Billy Wright**
1966 – 1976	**Bertie Mee**
1976 – 1983	**Terry Neill**
1984 – 1986	**Don Howe**
1986 – 1995	**George Graham**
1995 – 1996	**Bruce Rioch**
1996 –	**Arsène Wenger**

Arsenal in Europe

Year	Competition	P	W	D	L	F	A
1963–64	**Inter-Cities Fairs Cup**	4	1	1	2	11	8
1969–70	**Inter-Cities Fairs Cup**	12	8	2	2	23	6
1970–71	**Inter-Cities Fairs Cup**	8	4	2	2	12	5
1971–72	**European Cup**	6	4	0	2	13	4
1978–79	**UEFA Cup**	6	3	1	2	10	5
1979–80	**European Cup-Winners' Cup**	9	4	5	0	13	5
1981–82	**UEFA Cup**	4	3	0	1	5	2
1982–83	**UEFA Cup**	2	0	0	2	4	8
1991–92	**European Cup**	4	1	1	2	8	6
1993–94	**European Cup-Winners' Cup**	9	6	3	0	17	3
1994	**European Super Cup**	2	0	1	1	0	2
1994–95	**European Cup-Winners' Cup**	9	5	2	2	18	12
1996–97	**UEFA Cup**	2	0	0	2	2	4
1997–98	**UEFA Cup**	2	0	1	1	1	2
1998–99	**UEFA Champions League**	6	2	2	2	8	8
1999–2000	**UEFA Champions League**	6	2	2	2	9	9
1999–2000	**UEFA Cup**	9	6	2	1	21	9
2000–01	**UEFA Champions League**	14	7	3	4	19	18
2001–02	**UEFA Champions League**	12	5	1	6	17	17
2002–03	**UEFA Champions League**	12	4	5	3	15	9
2003–04	**UEFA Champions League**	10	5	2	3	16	11
2004–05	**UEFA Champions League**	8	3	4	1	13	9
2005–06	**UEFA Champions League**	13	8	4	1	15	4
2006–07	**UEFA Champions League**	10	5	3	2	13	6
2007–08	**UEFA Champions League**	12	7	3	2	24	9
2008–09	**UEFA Champions League**	14	7	3	4	23	11
2009–10	**UEFA Champions League**	12	7	2	3	26	14
2010–11	**UEFA Champions League**	8	5	0	3	21	11
2011–12	**UEFA Champions League**	10	6	2	2	13	11
2012–13	**UEFA Champions League**	8	4	1	3	13	11

Seaman's soapy ratio

David Seaman kept 237 clean sheets during his 564 appearances for Arsenal – a clean-sheet ratio of 42%.

Henry's trusty right foot

Of Thierry Henry's first 186 goals for the Club, the strikes that secured his place as top scorer, 110 were scored in the Premier League with his right foot.

Captain Marvel

The Arsenal captain who has made most appearances for the Club is Tony Adams with 669 games.

Tall story

Per Mertesacker is the tallest player to appear for Arsenal: he stands at 6ft 6in.

Musical Gooners

- Tony Adams and Gilles Grimandi both play the piano.
- Ian Wright and Charlie George have both recorded pop songs.
- Gilberto plays guitar, while his fellow Brazilian Julio Baptista plays the ukelele.
- Lee Dixon plays the drums.
- David Seaman won *Strictly Ice Dancing* on the BBC and appeared in *Dancing On Ice*.

Premier league hat-tricks

Date	Player	Opposition	Venue
11.9.93	**Kevin Campbell**	Ipswich Town (4)	Highbury
27.12.93	**Kevin Campbell**	Swindon Town	Highbury
5.3.94	**Ian Wright**	Ipswich Town	Portman Road
1.3.94	**Ian Wright**	Southampton	The Dell
1.4.95	**Ian Wright**	Ipswich Town	Highbury
16.9.96	**Ian Wright**	Sheffield Wednesday	Highbury
27.8.97	**Dennis Bergkamp**	Leicester City	Filbert Street
13.9.97	**Ian Wright**	Bolton Wanderers	Highbury
20.2.99	**Nicolas Anelka**	Leicester City	Highbury
23.10.99	**Nwankwo Kanu**	Chelsea	Stamford Bridge
21.11.99	**Marc Overmars**	Middlesbrough	Highbury
10.12.00	**Ray Parlour**	Newcastle United	Highbury
26.12.00	**Thierry Henry**	Leicester City	Highbury
3.3.01	**Sylvain Wiltord**	West Ham United	Highbury
19.1.03	**Thierry Henry**	West Ham United	Highbury
7.5.03	**Jermaine Pennant**	Southampton	Highbury
7.5.03	**Robert Pires**	Southampton	Highbury
11.5.03	**Freddie Ljungberg**	Sunderland	Stadium of Light
19.4.04	**Thierry Henry**	Liverpool	Highbury
16.4.04	**Thierry Henry** (4)	Leeds United	Highbury
5.3.05	**Thierry Henry**	Portsmouth	Highbury
2.4.05	**Thierry Henry**	Norwich City	Highbury
14.1.06	**Thierry Henry**	Middlesbrough	Highbury
7.5.06	**Thierry Henry**	Wigan Athletic	Highbury
22.9.07	**Emmanuel Adebayor**	Derby County	Emirates
28.4.08	**Emmanuel Adebayor**	Derby County	Pride Park
13.9.08	**Emmanuel Adebayor**	Blackburn Rovers	Ewood Park
21.4.09	**Andrey Arshavin** (4)	Liverpool	Anfield
21.8.10	**Theo Walcott**	Blackpool	Emirates
22.1.11	**Robin van Persie**	Wigan Athletic	Emirates
29.10.11	**Robin van Persie**	Chelsea	Stamford Bridge
4.2.12	**Robin van Persie**	Blackburn Rovers	Emirates
17.12.12	**Santi Cazorla**	Reading	Madejski Stadium
29.12.12	**Theo Walcott**	Newcastle United	Emirates

Short and sweet

Pat Rice was manager for just 14 days in September 1996.

The Welsh Wonder

Wales might have only reached one World Cup finals tournament to date but when they did, in 1958, Gunner Dave Bowen was their captain.

Chapman's chair

Herbert Chapman was a religious man. After his death his local church in Yorkshire presented the Club with the chair he sat in during services. For several years it was located in the boardroom, before being moved to the Club's museum.

Cliff Bastin's England goals

Date	Opposition and score
3 May 1933	England 1, Italy 1
20 May 1933	England 4, Switzerland 0 (two goals)
14 Apr 1934	England 3, Scotland 0
6 Feb 1935	England 2, Northern Ireland 1 (two goals)
4 Dec 1935	England 3, Germany 0
17 Oct 1936	England 1, Wales 2
18 Nov 1936	England 3, Northern Ireland 1
14 May 1938	England 6, Germany 3
21 May 1938	England 1, Switzerland 2
26 May 1938	England 4, France 2

Arsène's anniversary comestibles

The Club knocked 25% off the prices of hand-filled pies for the match which marked Arsène Wenger's tenth anniversary as Gunners boss.

Arsenal's 1,000th Premier League goal

Emmanuel Adebayor scored Arsenal's 1,000th Premier League goal, against Reading on 12 November 2007.

Henry outscores Sunderland

In the 2005–06 season, Thierry Henry scored more goals than the entire Sunderland squad managed. He struck 27 times, while Sunderland collectively scored 26.

Clocking in

The Arsenal clock graced Highbury for over 70 years. It was instigated by the great innovator Herbert Chapman, and the South Stand soon became known as the Clock End. When the Club moved to Emirates Stadium, the original clock changed homes too and now sits on the outside of the stadium, facing the Clock End Bridge as a symbolic reminder of Arsenal's time at Highbury.

Gunner Becks?

Arsène Wenger admits he would have loved to have signed David Beckham, who occasionally trained with Arsenal while with LA Galaxy to keep fit during the MLS close season

Arsenal's 10 biggest wins over Tottenham

Result	Date	Competition
Spurs 0, Arsenal 6	6/3/1935	League
Spurs 0, Arsenal 5	23/12/1978	League
Arsenal 5, Spurs 1	20/10/1934	League
Arsenal 4, Spurs 0	16/9/1967	League
Arsenal 4, Spurs 0	7/2/1953	League
Spurs 0, Arsenal 4	7/5/1927	League
Arsenal 5, Spurs 2	17/11/2012	League
Arsenal 5, Spurs 2	26/2/2012	League
Spurs 1, Arsenal 4	21/9/2010	League Cup
Spurs 1, Arsenal 4	31/1/1959	League

Bags of experience

The oldest player to appear for Arsenal is Jock Rutherford, who was 41 years, 159 days, when he turned out against Manchester City on 20 March 1926. The oldest Premier League appearance maker is John Lukic, who was 39 years, 336 days when he appeared against Derby County on 11 November 2000.

Double derby delight

Arsenal beat rivals Tottenham Hotspur twice in eight days in 2001. The first was a 2–0 league win on 31 March 2001, the second came on 8 April in the FA Cup semi-final, which the Gunners won 2–1.

Clean sheets in Europe

Arsenal have the record of keeping a clean sheet for 10 consecutive Champions League matches. They went exactly 995 minutes without conceding a goal.

Re (and re, and re, and re, and re) play

No less than five matches were needed to separate Arsenal and Sheffield Wednesday in the FA Cup in the 1978–79 season.

International honours

Thierry Henry, Emmanuel Petit, Robert Pires, Patrick Vieira and Sylvain Wiltord (of France) and Cesc Fabregas (of Spain) are the Gunners most decorated at international level. Each of these players have won both the World Cup and European Championship.

Blue for the Red

There is a blue English heritage plaque outside the house in Hendon once lived in by Herbert Chapman.

Jack's the lad

The Club was the first to pay a five-figure transfer fee when it spent £10,890 for David Jack in October 1928.

First match in the UEFA Champions League

v RC Lens (away) – 16 September 1998
Drew 1–1 (Overmars)

Out of this world

Space scientist and Gunners fan Ian P. Griffin named an asteroid after manager Arsène Wenger in 1998.

Gunners to Hammers

Ian Wright, Davor Suker and Nigel Winterburn all moved from Arsenal to West Ham United between 1998 and 2000.

Bolton double

Arsenal played Bolton twice in three days in January 2010. Both were Premier League fixtures and the Gunners won both encounters, the first finished 2–0 and the second was a 4–2 win.

The 49-match unbeaten run

	Played	Won	Drawn	Lost	For	Against	Points
Home	25	20	5	0	63	21	65
Away	24	16	8	0	49	14	56
Overall	49	36	13	0	112	35	121

High at home

The highest home attendance for a Gunners match came against Sunderland in March 1935. The total present was 73,295.

Team of the century

Arsenal were the team of the 20th century, according to a table based on the average league finishes of clubs between 1900 and 1999. The Club's average league position was 8.5, a whisker ahead of Liverpool's at 8.7.

Arsenal centurions

Name	Goals	Games	100th goal game
Thierry Henry	228	377	181
Ian Wright	185	288	143
Cliff Bastin	178	396	174
John Radford	149	481	306
Jimmy Brain	139	232	144
Ted Drake	139	184	108
Doug Lishman	137	244	163
Robin van Persie	132	278	238
Joe Hulme	125	374	307
David Jack	124	208	156
Dennis Bergkamp	120	423	296
Reg Lewis	118	176	152
Alan Smith	115	347	251
Jack Lambert	109	161	149
Frank Stapleton	108	300	276
David Herd	107	180	165
Joe Baker	100	156	152

The Ox (senior)

Alex Oxlade-Chamberlain's father Mark Chamberlain played for England and appeared in the match against Brazil during which John Barnes scored his famous wonder goal. When history repeated itself in England's 2013 friendly against Brazil, dad missed the Ox's spectacular goal because he fell asleep in front of the telly!

Global Gunners

Twelve different nationalities scored for Arsenal in the Premier League during the 2007–08 season.

Cup totals

Arsenal played 59 FA Cup ties during the 1970s. In the 1880s they played just four.

The horse and the guinea pigs

Andrey Arshavin says he has a recurring dream that he is a horse in a field surrounded by guinea pigs.

A matter of percentages

Arsenal won 55% of their Premier League games during the 2012–13 campaign.

Abou the builder

Gunners player Abou Diaby ceremonially put in place the first of Emirates Stadium's 60,000 seats.

Arsène's derby delight

Arsène Wenger lost just one of the first 21 north London derbies of his reign.

Arsenal at the movies

The Arsenal Stadium Mystery
This 1939 "whodunnit" was set in Highbury.
Fever Pitch
A 1997 dramatisation of author Nick Hornby's bestseller about life as an Arsenal fan.
The Baby Juice Express
Both Ray Parlour and David Seaman make cameo appearances in this 2001 flick.
Plunkett and Macleane
In this 1999 highway film are two characters called Dixon and Winterburn. Hmm, wonder where they got the inspiration for those names?
Lamb
The old North Bank of Highbury features in this 1985 film, which stars Liam Neeson.

A UK-free zone

On 2 February 2005 Arsenal became the first club in English football history to field a squad with no UK-born players. The opponents were Crystal Palace.

The 49-match unbeaten run in full

Season 2002–03

1 Arsenal 6–1 Southampton, 7 May 2003
2 Sunderland 0–4 Arsenal, 11 May 2003

Season 2003–04

3 Arsenal 2–1 Everton, 16 Aug 2003
4 Middlesbrough 0–4 Arsenal, 24 Aug 2003
5 Arsenal 2–0 Aston Villa, 27 Aug 2003
6 Man City 1–2 Arsenal, 31 Aug 2003
7 Arsenal 1–1 Portsmouth, 13 Sept 2003
8 Man Utd 0–0 Arsenal, 21 Sept 2003
9 Arsenal 3–2 Newcastle, 26 Sept 2003
10 Liverpool 1–2 Arsenal, 4 Oct 2003
11 Arsenal 2–1 Chelsea, 18 Oct 2003
12 Charlton 1–1 Arsenal, 26 Oct 2003
13 Leeds 1–4 Arsenal, 1 Nov 2003
14 Arsenal 2–1 Tottenham, 8 Nov 2003
15 Birmingham 0–3 Arsenal, 22 Nov 2003
16 Arsenal 0–0 Fulham, 30 Nov 2003
17 Leicester 1–1 Arsenal, 6 Dec 2003
18 Arsenal 1–0 Blackburn, 14 Dec 2003
19 Bolton 1–1 Arsenal, 20 Dec 2003
20 Arsenal 3–0 Wolves, 26 Dec 2003
21 Southampton 0–1 Arsenal, 29 Dec 2003
22 Everton 1–1 Arsenal, 7 Jan 2004
23 Arsenal 4–1 Middlesbrough, 10 Jan 2004
24 Aston Villa 0–2 Arsenal, 18 Jan 2004
25 Arsenal 2–1 Man City, 1 Jan 2004

26 Wolves 1–3 Arsenal, 7 Feb 2004
27 Arsenal 2–0 Southampton, 10 Feb 2004
28 Chelsea 1–2 Arsenal, 21 Feb 2004
29 Arsenal 2–1 Charlton, 28 Feb 2004
30 Blackburn 0–2 Arsenal, 13 March 2004
31 Arsenal 2–1 Bolton, 20 Mar 2004
32 Arsenal 1–1 Man Utd, 28 Mar 2004
33 Arsenal 4–2 Liverpool, 9 Apr 2004
34 Newcastle 0–0 Arsenal, 11 Apr 2004
35 Arsenal 5–0 Leeds, 16 Apr 2004
36 Tottenham 2–2 Arsenal, 25 Apr 2004
37 Arsenal 0–0 Birmingham, 1 May 2004
38 Portsmouth 1–1 Arsenal, 4 May 2004
39 Fulham 0–1 Arsenal, 9 May 2004
40 Arsenal 2–1 Leicester, 15 May 2004

Season 2004–05

41 Everton 1–4 Arsenal, 15 Aug 2004
42 Arsenal 5–3 Middlesbrough, 22 Aug 2004
43 Arsenal 3–0 Blackburn, 25 Aug 2004
44 Norwich 1–4 Arsenal, 28 Aug 2004
45 Fulham 0–3 Arsenal, 11 Sept 2004
46 Arsenal 2–2 Bolton, 18 Sept 2004
47 Man City 0–1 Arsenal, 25 Sept 2004
48 Arsenal 4–0 Charlton, 2 Oct 2004
49 Arsenal 3–1 Aston Villa, 16 Oct 2004

	Played	Won	Drawn	Lost	For	Against	Points
Home	25	20	5	0	63	21	65
Away	24	16	8	0	49	14	56
Overall	49	36	13	0	112	35	21

Most-capped England internationals

Ashley Cole	101
Kenny Sansom	77
David Seaman	75
Sol Campbell	73
Alan Ball	72
Tony Adams	66
David Platt	62
Martin Keown	43
Paul Mariner	35
Ian Wright	33
Theo Walcott	31
Eddie Hapgood	30
Lee Dixon	22
Paul Merson	21
Wilf Copping	20

Low turnout

The lowest Premier League attendance in Arsenal history came against Wimbledon in February 1993. Just 18,253 attended.

Perfect pizza

Patrick Vieira's favourite pizza topping is pepperoni. Theo Walcott's is four cheeses.

First against Fosse

The first match played at Arsenal Stadium (Highbury) was against Leicester Fosse in 1913. Arsenal won 2–1.

Tony and Viv forever

Tony Woodcock and Viv Anderson played together for Nottingham Forest and Arsenal. After retiring, they went into business together.

A Wright softie!

When Ian Wright wants to cry he watches the movie *Beaches*, featuring Bette Midler.

Theo's books

Theo Walcott has four published children's books – *T.J. and the Hat-Trick*, *T.J. and the Penalty*, *T.J. and the Winning Goal* and *T.J. and the Cup Run*. The eponymous T.J. is the new kid on the block who hooks up with a bunch of football-mad classmates to star in the school football team. Sound like anyone you know! He also published his memoirs in 2011, *Theo: Growing Up Fast*.

Arsène Wenger's season-by-season Premier League record

Season	P	W	D	L	F	A	Win%	GPG	CPG
1996–97	36	16	11	9	56	33	44.44	1.56	0.92
1997–98	54	33	13	8	89	46	61.11	1.65	0.85
1998–99	54	31	15	8	84	38	57.41	1.56	0.70
1999–2000	59	33	11	15	112	66	55.93	1.90	1.12
2000–01	59	32	13	14	99	62	54.24	1.68	1.05
2001–02	60	39	11	10	119	62	65.00	1.98	1.03
2002–03	59	34	15	10	119	58	57.63	2.02	0.98
2003–04	59	38	14	7	114	48	64.41	1.93	0.81
2004–05	57	37	13	7	117	51	64.91	2.05	0.89
2005–06	59	33	11	15	96	43	55.93	1.63	0.73
2006–07	59	30	17	12	98	53	50.85	1.66	0.90
2007–08	58	36	15	7	113	52	62.07	1.95	0.90
2008–09	61	33	16	12	113	54	54.10	1.85	0.89
2009–10	55	33	8	14	116	63	60.00	2.11	1.15
2010–11	58	31	13	14	119	64	53.45	2.05	1.10
2011–12	54	31	9	14	96	67	57.41	1.78	1.24
2012–13	53	29	12	12	105	60	54.72	1.98	1.13
Total	954	549	217	188	1765	920	57.55	1.85	0.96

A perfect 10

Arsenal went unbeaten for the final 10 matches of the 2012–13 season, which helped them qualify for the Champions League for the 16th successive season. The Club finished top of the Fair Play League for the season. The Ladies Team won the 2013 FA Women's Cup – the 12th time they have lifted the trophy.

200 not out

It took Arsène Wenger just 398 matches to collect 200 wins as Gunners boss.

A concrete fact

Over 60,000 cubic metres of concrete were used to build Emirates Stadium.

Saint Santi

Santi Cazorla was named the Arsenal.com official player of the season for 2012–13 – his debut campaign in the English game. The versatile Spaniard made 47 starts and scored 12 times for the Gunners.

Speedy Theo

Theo Walcott scored the 2012–13 campaign's fastest goal, netting after just 20 seconds at QPR in May.

Baby love

In 2006, some 36 babies around the world were named Arsenal.

CHAPTER 2

The Great Managers

Arsène Wenger is only the 19th manager in Arsenal's illustrious history that now stretches over 125 years. The Club has been built on the stability that comes with placing faith in our managers and giving them the freedom to manage the team.

In this chapter we look at six of the men who have been handed the responsibility to take charge of the players who have graced the pitches for Arsenal and the emotions of the millions of supporters from around the world who follow the Club.

George Morrell, who managed the team from 1908 to 1915, does not make our six of the best but deserves a mention for being in charge at a time when the club set up home at Highbury in 1913. He was succeeded by Leslie Knighton, who subsequently made way, after six years, for the legendary Herbert Chapman.

The innovative Yorkshireman had such an influence on the club a bronze bust was cast in his image and it stood proudly in the marble halls of Highbury until it was moved to a place of similar stature in our new home around the corner at Ashburton Grove.

Other memorable greats followed in Chapman's footsteps and their exploits are chronicled here, including some interesting facts and figures to illuminate their spells in charge.

Only one other boss has been so successful and influential that the Club has had his likeness preserved in bronze and that is Wenger. Where does he rank in your list of Arsenal's greatest managers? Have a read and make an informed decision…

Herbert Chapman

"There is one golden rule: it is never safe to be satisfied," was the principal by which Herbert Chapman led his groundbreaking managerial career.

It was a career which not only transformed Arsenal, but football across the country and ultimately the world throughout the 1920s and '30s before his sudden death.

In addition to an incredible trophy haul during his time at Highbury, Chapman is regarded as one of the game's very first visionaries, who championed innovations such as floodlights, shirt numbers and cross-continent competition.

He is also regarded by many as the inventor of modern football tactics, with an emphasis on a strong, compact defence with quick forwards. It has even been suggested that the Yorkshireman constructed the world's first tactics board, a table top painted green.

Although Chapman was already highly rated after successful spells in charge at Northampton, Leeds and Huddersfield, where he won back-to-back titles, Henry Norris could never have imagined the revolution his appointment was about to inspire in north London.

His first season, 1925–26, brought Arsenal the highest-place finish in their history and by 1930, a first FA Cup was in the trophy cabinet. It would be the prelude to a decade of dominance for the Club.

Fronted by little-known teenager Cliff Bastin, who Chapman plucked from Exeter in 1929, Arsenal secured the 1931 Division 1 title with a record points total of 66.

It was around this time that the manager began to lobby for Gillespie Road, the tube station behind Highbury, to be renamed Arsenal. "Whoever heard of Gillespie Road," he famously said. "It is Arsenal around here." And his wish was granted on Bonfire Night, 1932, when the name was officially changed – and Arsenal remain the only club in the capital with a tube station named after them.

On the pitch, there were more fireworks. Another title followed in 1933 before tragedy struck six months later, with his side closing in on their second successive crown. After watching the Arsenal third team face Guildford nursing a cold in January 1934, Chapman's condition worsened on his return home. And on 6 January 1934, aged just 55, one of history's greatest managers died at his house in Hendon.

In his memory, Arsenal did go on to secure the title that season – and made it a hat-trick in 1935, with an FA Cup arriving 12 months later. The final act of that great Chapman team was to mark the penultimate season before the outbreak of the Second World War by winning Division 1 for the fifth time in eight years in 1938.

Even Chapman himself might have been satisfied.

DID YOU KNOW THAT?
Herbert Chapman's playing career ended with a spell for Tottenham Hotspur, who he joined for £70 in 1905.

George Allison

George Allison's career was remarkable. It started when he was a journalist reporting on the Club, and he went on to become Arsenal's programme editor, Club historian, member of the board of directors, secretary and finally manager during a 41-year association with the cCub.

Allison guided the Club shrewdly through two incredibly difficult periods: following the death of Herbert Chapman in January 1934, and through the Second World War.

Allison's background in journalism meant he was the perfect figurehead for the Club, dealing well with both the press and the public.

Yet he acknowledged he did not have the same football knowledge as Chapman; for example, so much of the work with the players was actually taken care of by Joe Shaw and Tom Whittaker, with the three men forming a hugely effective triumvirate.

Shaw was the favourite to succeed Chapman after the latter's death but he was not keen on being in the limelight, which meant that this rather unusual arrangement was the best solution for all concerned.

It certainly worked, as Arsenal won the league in 1933–34 and then, once Allison had been appointed permanently that summer, went on to win two more league titles and an FA Cup before the outbreak of war in 1939.

That was in part due to the decision to sign Ted Drake, one of the most legendary forwards in Arsenal's history.

Drake scored seven times against Aston Villa in 1935 – away from home, and from just nine shots – a top-flight record that still stands, but Arsenal dipped slightly during the latter half of the 1930s.

Their finishes before the war were sixth, third, first and fifth, far from disastrous but still not as impressive as in the previous decade, although the 1936 FA Cup victory allayed that somewhat.

That victory, over Second Division side Sheffield United, was sealed by a goal from Drake – a strike made all the more remarkable by the fact that the forward had barely recovered from a cartilage operation and was forced to leave the field immediately after scoring.

And the manner of Arsenal and Allison's victory in the 1936–37 Championship race was also highly dramatic. Wolves went into the final day knowing victory at Sunderland would enable them to win the title, but they fell to a shock 1–0 defeat, allowing Arsenal to ease past them after they beat Bolton 5–0 at Highbury.

Yet the war ensured Arsenal had no official first-class matches for six long years.

Allison helped Arsenal win the London League, the League South and the League South Cup during that time, but his main task was to ensure the club was still alive once the war had finished.

That he did, but in the summer of 1947 he retired, declaring that he desired "a less strenuous life" away from the Club.

DID YOU KNOW THAT?

George Allison commentated on the first ever FA Cup final to be broadcast on the radio, between Arsenal and Cardiff City in 1927, despite being a member of the board of directors at Highbury.

Tom Whittaker

Tom Whittaker's early retirement from playing aged just 27 proved hugely important in the development of Arsenal over the next 30 years.

Able to play in defence, midfield or attack, Whittaker spent six years as an Arsenal player before a knee injury led to him being appointed assistant trainer in 1926.

Whittaker – who also took charge of all medical duties at the Club – succeeded George Hardy as trainer in February 1927 and built up a reputation as the finest coach in the game, serving Arsenal with distinction under Herbert Chapman and then George Allison.

He was the obvious successor to succeed Allison when he decided to step down as manager in 1947.

Arsenal had narrowly avoided relegation the previous season, but Whittaker's decision to sign Joe Mercer and Ronnie Rooke proved inspired.

Aged 32 and 35, respectively, Mercer and Rooke were both thought to be well past their best. Yet Rooke scored 29 goals in 28 league games and Mercer was inspirational as he succeeded Les Compton as captain due to the latter's cricket commitments with Middlesex.

Arsenal led the league from the first day to the last, yet they found out they were champions in unusual fashion. A draw at Leeds was not enough to clinch the title, but at Doncaster station on the way home Denis Compton bought a paper and was delighted to read Manchester United, Burnley and Derby County had all lost – meaning Arsenal could not be caught at the top of the table.

Whittaker turned down a chance to rebuild Torino, the Italian giants whose side was decimated by an air disaster in 1950, and then led Arsenal to an FA Cup victory over Liverpool.

Reg Lewis scored both goals in the final as Arsenal made the most of a kind draw – they were at home in every round and, as they faced Chelsea at White Hart Lane in the semi-finals they never left London – to take the cup.

Two years later Whittaker's side put in a brave performance as their ten-men lost to Newcastle after an early injury reduced their numbers, but in 1953 he secured Arsenal's seventh league title.

It was an astonishingly close title race between Arsenal and Preston, one that the Londoners won on goal average. If goal difference had been used then Arsenal would have finished on +33 to Preston's +25, but after they finished equal on points Arsenal's goal average of 1.516 was superior to Preston's 1.417.

Yet a great team was ageing by that point, and that proved to be a last hurrah. Whittaker attempted to build another side, but without success.

He was eventually ordered to take a complete rest due to nervous exhaustion, but he died of a heart attack in October 1956.

DID YOU KNOW THAT?
Tom Whittaker won an MBE for secret work in connection with the D-Day landings during the Second World War.

Bertie Mee

Bertie Mee arrived at Arsenal as a physiotherapist in 1960 and left 16 years later as one of the most decorated managers in the Club's history.

When he made the transition from the treatment room to the dressing room, there was widespread shock – with few as surprised as the man himself. Put simply, the side were in the doldrums when he was appointed in 1966.

After the success of the 1930s and – to a lesser extent – the '40s, Arsenal were without a trophy since 1953 and in desperate need of rejuvenation.

Few thought a physiotherapist – with little pedigree as a player – could do it, and even Mee could see his potential shortcomings. One of his first acts as manager was to recruit Don Howe and Dave Sexton as his assistants.

The pair of former players, then in their thirties, went on to become two of the finest coaches this country has ever produced.

It proved a masterstroke by Mee, who was a sergeant in the Royal Army Medical Corps during the Second World War, as he and his team of coaches set about transforming the Arsenal.

It took him just two years to steer the Gunners to a final, in the League Cup, which they lost. And, although the same thing happened 12 months later, it was clear to see that Arsenal were truly back in contention.

Then, in the following season, he led his side to glory in the Fairs Cup – the Club's first European honour and a remarkable win over crack Belgian side Anderlecht featuring a 3–0 win at Highbury to overturn a 3–1 first leg deficit.

But it only got better for Mee's Arsenal in the following season with an historic Double clinched in the perfect circumstances.

Ray Kennedy headed the only goal of the game at the home of Arsenal's arch-rivals Tottenham to secure a 1–0 win, and the first league title under Mee. It was the climax of a remarkable run of 11 wins from their final 13 games, beating favourites Leeds to the crown by a single point.

And the fabled League and Cup "Double" was clinched on the following weekend beneath Wembley's famous Twin Towers when Charlie George scored the extra-time winner against Liverpool to take the FA Cup back to Highbury.

Sadly, Mee failed to reach those heights after 1971, resigned five years later and never held a managing post again. But his place in the Club's folklore is unquestionable having been the first European and Double-winning manager at Highbury.

And, although much-maligned for a lack of tactical nous, no Arsenal manager before Arsène Wenger managed more than his 241 wins in charge, and he was made an OBE for his services to football in 1984.

Not bad for a physio.

DID YOU KNOW THAT?

Before joining Arsenal as physio, Mee worked as a remedial gymnast with disabled soldiers.

George Graham

George Graham was involved in one of the most dramatic title finishes in football, but he will also be remembered for building a defence to serve the Club for over a decade and long after his reign.

The crowning glory came at Anfield on 26 May 1989 when Michael Thomas hit the winner in injury time to bring the Division 1 title back to Highbury for the first time since 1971.

Remarkably, Graham had been part of that Double-winning side as a player and here he was again leading Arsenal to the title.

With the Club struggling to win any kind of silverware in the 1980s, Arsenal turned their attentions to the Scotsman who had shown great promise at Millwall.

Graham wasted no time implementing his ideas at the north London Club and installed a strong discipline and work ethic among his players.

They say in football that you should build your team from the back but Graham took that to another level and started laying the foundations for one of the most successful backlines in English football.

Young captain Tony Adams was the foundation and he blended in the likes of Martin Keown, Lee Dixon, Steve Bould and Nigel Winterburn to play alongside him. The star keepers were John Lukic and David Seaman. Young talents such as Paul Merson, David Rocastle and Michael Thomas would also become legends under Graham.

Arsenal came fourth in Graham's first season, but more importantly they won their first trophy since 1979, as the Club – with Charlie Nicholas scoring twice – came from behind and beat Liverpool in the League Cup final.

That just gave Graham the appetite to want more success and a second title followed in the 1990–91 season at the cost of just ONE defeat.

Another major signing was to arrive the following season as Ian Wright made his way into the Arsenal dressing-room and he soon wrote his name into the record books as he became the leading goalscorer in the Club's history before being eclipsed by Thierry Henry.

Graham's Arsenal became the first club ever to win the FA Cup and League Cup "Double" in 1993. And perhaps a greater feat was a first European trophy in 24 years when Alan Smith's goal beat Parma in the European Cup-Winners' Cup to define the "one-nil to the Arsenal" era.

Despite his dismissal 10 months later, Graham had put Arsenal firmly back on the footballing map and many of his players would enjoy continued success under Arsène Wenger.

DID YOU KNOW THAT?
When Graham ended his playing career in his early thirties, his first coaching role was under Terry Venables at Crystal Palace.

Arsène Wenger

Arsène Wenger has transformed the Club following his arrival in October 1996. Some sing "he wears a magic hat" in awe of what the master tactician has brought to the Arsenal.

Wenger is quite simply the greatest manager in the Club's history and the longest serving too in a record-breaking run. The French coach has managed to secure more victories, deliver a higher win ratio and win more trophies than any of his predecessors.

It is hard to believe that he was a relative unknown when he first arrived at Highbury and question marks were raised over his appointment. But he quickly showed why David Dein and the Arsenal board rated him so highly with his innovative methods of getting the best out of his players both on and off the pitch.

He wasted no time bringing major silverware to the club as he managed to win the Double in his first full season. The influx of French players such as Patrick Vieira and Emmanuel Petit changed the philosophy within the Club and Wenger's tactical knowledge was obvious.

Another Double followed once again in 2002. And it was not just the way Arsenal won, but the brand of football they were playing with Dennis Bergkamp and Thierry Henry supreme.

It was the French coach who brought Henry to Arsenal and turned him from a winger into the all-time leading goalscorer in the Club's history. And it all came together in the 2003–04 campaign when his philosophy reached its peak as Arsenal went an entire season unbeaten, with his team labelled the "Invincibles".

No other team in the modern era has achieved the same feat. Wenger stated at the time that it left his Arsenal "immortal". The league success was even more special as Arsenal managed to win the title at Tottenham's White Hart Lane.

Silverware continued to arrive as Wenger won his fourth FA Cup in 2005 following a penalty shoot-out victory over Manchester United at the Millennium Stadium.

After steering the Club to the 2006 Champions League final, Wenger suffered heartache as he saw Barcelona come from behind to score two goals in the last 14 minutes in Paris.

Despite the lack of trophies in recent years, Wenger has continued to stamp his own brand of attacking football and helped to bring through the best young talent.

He was instrumental in helping the Club make a big move into Emirates Stadium and establishing a new state-of-the-art training ground, placing Arsenal at the forefront of world football.

All future Arsenal managers will be judged by his standards and few could argue he is one of the greatest ever coaches to have managed in England.

DID YOU KNOW THAT?

Arsène Wenger speaks five languages and has a master's degree in economics and sociology from Strasbourg University. He also has the Freedom of the Borough of Islington.

CHAPTER 3

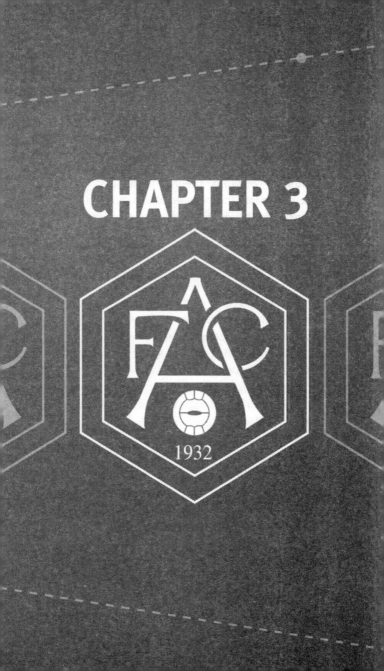

We Are the Champions

It is football's most inarguable achievement: to finish at the top of the league table at the end of the season. The league table does not lie, as the saying goes, so the team who finishes at the summit of the top flight can claim authoritatively to be the best in the land. Arsenal supporters have had the pleasure of this moment on 13 occasions during the Club's history.

Five of the league titles came during the glorious 1930s, as Herbert Chapman made his mark on the Club and on English football in general. After further championships during the 1940s, 50s and 70s, the remainder were won by two managers: George Graham and Arsène Wenger. Some of the Club's titles were won relatively comfortably, with the rest of the league able to do little more than look on as the Gunners galloped home. Others were more tightly fought affairs, which went to the wire.

In the coming chapter you can relive every one of these top-flight titles with notable moments and stand-out fixtures recalled alongside the final league table for the season in question. The players and managers who masterminded the glory are also fondly remembered.

Of course, all Gunners fans are hungry for the next instalment in this chapter, as Arsenal Football Club succeed in becoming crowned champions of England once again. As the squad and management work hard to bring that day closer, enjoy reading about the delights of times gone by.

Arsenal's first championship season included several statistical points of interest. Their records at home and away from home were identical: 14 wins, 5 draws and 2 defeats. Jack Lambert set a Club record with his 38 league goals, and the Gunners set a league record with an impressive 66-strong points haul. Their strongest challengers throughout the campaign were Aston Villa. At Highbury, Arsenal beat Villa 5–2, yet at Villa Park the Midlanders had their revenge, winning 5–1. Ultimately, the Gunners became the first side south of Birmingham to win the First Division title.

	P	W	D	L	F	A	W	D	L	F	A	Pts
1. Arsenal	**42**	**14**	**5**	**2**	**67**	**27**	**14**	**5**	**2**	**60**	**32**	**66**
2. Aston Villa	42	17	3	1	86	34	8	6	7	42	44	59
3. Sheffield Wednesday	42	14	3	4	65	32	8	5	8	37	43	52
4. Portsmouth	42	11	7	3	46	26	7	6	8	38	41	49
5. Huddersfield Town	42	10	8	3	45	27	8	4	9	36	38	48
6. Derby County	42	12	6	3	56	31	6	4	11	38	48	46
7. Middlesbrough	42	13	5	3	57	28	6	3	12	41	62	46
8. Manchester City	42	13	2	6	41	29	5	8	8	34	41	46
9. Liverpool	42	11	6	4	48	28	4	6	11	38	57	42
10. Blackburn Rovers	42	14	3	4	54	28	3	5	13	29	56	42
11. Sunderland	42	12	4	5	61	38	4	5	12	28	47	41
12. Chelsea	42	13	4	4	42	19	2	6	13	22	48	40
13. Grimsby Town	42	13	2	6	55	31	4	3	14	27	56	39
14. Bolton Wanderers	42	12	6	3	45	26	3	3	15	23	55	39
15. Sheffield United	42	10	7	4	49	31	4	3	14	29	53	38
16. Leicester City	42	12	4	5	50	38	4	2	15	30	57	38
17. Newcastle United	42	9	2	10	41	45	6	4	11	37	42	36
18. West Ham United	42	11	3	7	56	44	3	5	13	23	50	36
19. Birmingham City	42	11	3	7	37	28	2	7	12	18	42	36
20. Blackpool	42	8	7	6	41	44	3	3	15	30	81	32
21. Leeds United	42	10	3	8	49	31	2	4	15	19	50	31
22. Manchester United	42	6	6	9	30	37	1	2	18	23	78	22

1932–33

This campaign did not start favourably for the Gunners. They lost Charlie Jones through injury and faced defeat by West Bromwich Albion in the first home match of the season. However, they then embarked on an amazing run in which they took 32 out of 36 available points. The crowning match of that sequence was a 9–2 thrashing of Sheffield United on Christmas Eve. Aston Villa and Sheffield Wednesday continued to stake their own claim to the top spot but both lost at Highbury. Indeed, April saw Arsenal win five matches in a row. The last, a 3–1 win over Chelsea at Stamford Bridge, confirmed the Gunners as champions.

	P	W	D	L	F	A	W	D	L	F	A	Pts
1. Arsenal	**42**	**14**	**3**	**4**	**70**	**27**	**11**	**5**	**5**	**48**	**34**	**58**
2. Aston Villa	42	16	2	3	60	29	7	6	8	32	38	54
3. Sheffield Wednesday	42	15	5	1	46	20	6	4	11	34	48	51
4. West Bromwich Albion	42	16	1	4	50	23	4	8	9	33	47	49
5. Newcastle United	42	15	2	4	44	24	7	3	11	27	39	49
6. Huddersfield Town	42	11	6	4	32	17	7	5	9	34	36	47
7. Derby County	42	11	8	2	49	25	4	6	11	27	44	44
8. Leeds United	42	10	6	5	39	24	5	8	8	20	38	44
9. Portsmouth	42	14	3	4	39	22	4	4	13	35	54	43
10. Sheffield United	42	14	3	4	50	30	3	6	12	24	50	43
11. Everton	42	13	6	2	54	24	3	3	15	27	50	41
12. Sunderland	42	8	7	6	33	31	7	3	11	30	49	40
13. Birmingham City	42	13	3	5	40	23	1	8	12	17	34	39
14. Liverpool	42	10	6	5	53	33	4	5	12	26	51	39
15. Blackburn Rovers	42	11	6	4	48	41	3	4	14	28	61	38
16. Manchester City	42	12	3	6	47	30	4	2	15	21	41	37
17. Middlesbrough	42	8	5	8	35	33	6	4	11	28	40	37
18. Chelsea	42	9	4	8	38	29	5	3	13	25	44	35
19. Leicester City	42	9	9	3	43	25	2	4	15	32	64	35
20. Wolverhampton W.	42	10	4	7	56	48	3	5	13	24	48	35
21. Bolton Wanderers	42	10	7	4	49	33	2	2	17	29	59	33
22. Blackpool	42	11	2	8	44	35	3	3	15	25	50	33

Statistically, it is interesting to note that Arsenal scored just 75 goals all year, compared with 118 the previous season and 115 the season after. The injury to Alex James, who fell in the first match of the season against Birmingham, and the loss of Joe Hulme explain the team's comparatively low tally. This time, it was Derby County and Huddersfield Town who put up the strongest challenges. However, over Easter, Arsenal beat both teams in crucial ties to once more rise to and remain at the top. The tragic loss of Herbert Chapman, who died of pneumonia in January, deeply shook everyone at the Club.

	P	W	D	L	F	A	W	D	L	F	A	Pts
1. Arsenal	**42**	**15**	**4**	**2**	**45**	**19**	**10**	**5**	**6**	**30**	**28**	**59**
2. Huddersfield Town	42	16	3	2	53	19	7	7	7	37	42	56
3. Tottenham Hotspur	42	14	3	4	51	24	7	4	10	28	32	49
4. Derby County	42	11	8	2	45	22	6	3	12	23	32	45
5. Manchester City	42	14	4	3	50	29	3	7	11	15	43	45
6. Sunderland	42	14	6	1	57	17	2	6	13	24	39	44
7. West Bromwich Albion	42	12	4	5	49	28	5	6	10	29	42	44
8. Blackburn Rovers	42	16	5	0	57	21	2	2	17	17	60	43
9. Leeds United	42	13	5	3	52	21	4	3	14	23	45	42
10. Portsmouth	42	11	5	5	31	21	4	7	10	21	34	42
11. Sheffield Wednesday	42	9	5	7	33	24	7	4	10	29	43	41
12. Stoke City	42	11	5	5	33	19	4	6	11	25	52	41
13. Aston Villa	42	10	5	6	45	34	4	7	10	33	41	40
14. Everton	42	9	7	5	38	27	3	9	9	24	36	40
15. Wolverhampton W.	42	13	4	4	50	28	1	8	12	24	58	40
16. Middlesbrough	42	13	3	5	51	27	3	4	14	17	53	39
17. Leicester City	42	10	6	5	36	26	4	5	12	23	48	39
18. Liverpool	42	10	6	5	52	37	4	4	13	27	50	38
19. Chelsea	42	12	3	6	44	24	2	5	14	23	45	36
20. Birmingham City	42	8	6	7	29	20	4	6	11	25	36	36
21. Newcastle United	42	6	11	4	42	29	4	3	14	26	48	34
22. Sheffield United	42	11	5	5	40	25	1	2	18	18	76	31

1934–35

A season dominated by injuries saw Arsenal win only one match away from home until January – yet the Gunners still finished the campaign as champions. A major force in this was new signing Ted Drake, who scored a record 42 goals. That tally included four matches in which he scored four goals and three in which he scored three. The season had started on a high with an 8–1 demolition of Liverpool. It was not until March that Arsenal were knocked off top spot, when Sunderland went a point ahead. But by the time Arsenal had played their games in hand they had wrestled back the lead, opening up a four-point gap at the summit.

	P	W	D	L	F	A	W	D	L	F	A	Pts
1. Arsenal	**42**	**15**	**4**	**2**	**74**	**17**	**8**	**8**	**5**	**41**	**29**	**58**
2. Sunderland	42	13	4	4	57	24	6	12	3	33	27	54
3. Sheffield Wednesday	42	14	7	0	42	17	4	6	11	28	47	49
4. Manchester City	42	13	5	3	53	25	7	3	11	29	42	48
5. Grimsby Town	42	13	6	2	49	25	4	5	12	29	35	45
6. Derby County	42	10	4	7	44	28	8	5	8	37	38	45
7. Liverpool	42	13	4	4	53	29	6	3	12	32	59	45
8. Everton	42	14	5	2	64	32	2	7	12	25	56	44
9. West Bromwich Albion	42	10	8	3	55	33	7	2	12	28	50	44
10. Stoke City	42	12	5	4	46	20	6	1	14	25	50	42
11. Preston North End	42	11	5	5	33	22	4	7	10	29	45	42
12. Chelsea	42	11	5	5	49	32	5	4	12	24	50	41
13. Aston Villa	42	11	6	4	50	36	3	7	11	24	52	41
14. Portsmouth	42	10	5	6	41	24	5	5	11	30	48	40
15. Blackburn Rovers	42	12	5	4	42	23	2	6	13	24	55	39
16. Huddersfield Town	42	11	5	5	52	27	3	5	13	24	44	38
17. Wolverhampton W.	42	13	3	5	65	38	2	5	14	23	56	38
18. Leeds United	42	10	6	5	48	35	3	6	12	27	57	38
19. Birmingham City	42	10	3	8	36	36	3	7	11	27	45	36
20. Middlesbrough	42	8	9	4	38	29	2	5	14	32	61	34
21. Leicester City	42	9	4	8	39	30	3	5	13	22	56	33
22. Tottenham Hotspur	42	8	8	5	34	31	2	2	17	20	62	30

The season in which the Club won its fifth title in eight years was inconsistent and frustrating at times. Cliff Bastin and George Male were the main survivors from the golden years in which the Gunners won a hat-trick of titles. New names such as Mel Griffiths and Eddie Carr came to the fore and helped the team overcome confident challenges from Brentford, Wolves and Preston. The destiny of the title went down to the last day of the season. The Gunners beat Bolton 5–0 at Highbury but they needed Sunderland to deny victory to Wolves to guarantee the top spot. Fortunately, the north-Easterners did just that.

	P	W	D	L	F	A	W	D	L	F	A	Pts
1. Arsenal	**42**	**15**	**4**	**2**	**52**	**16**	**6**	**6**	**9**	**25**	**28**	**52**
2. Wolverhampton W.	42	11	8	2	47	21	9	3	9	25	28	51
3. Preston North End	42	9	9	3	34	21	7	8	6	30	23	49
4. Charlton Athletic	42	14	5	2	43	14	2	9	10	22	37	46
5. Middlesbrough	42	12	4	5	40	26	7	4	10	32	39	46
6. Brentford	42	10	6	5	44	27	8	3	10	25	32	45
7. Bolton Wanderers	42	11	6	4	38	22	4	9	8	26	38	45
8. Sunderland	42	12	6	3	32	18	2	10	9	23	39	44
9. Leeds United	42	11	6	4	38	26	3	9	9	26	43	43
10. Chelsea	42	11	6	4	40	22	3	7	11	25	43	41
11. Liverpool	42	9	5	7	40	30	6	6	9	25	41	41
12. Blackpool	42	10	5	6	33	26	6	3	12	28	40	40
13. Derby County	42	10	5	6	42	36	5	5	11	24	51	40
14. Everton	42	11	5	5	54	34	5	2	14	25	41	39
15. Huddersfield Town	42	11	3	7	29	24	6	2	13	26	44	39
16. Leicester City	42	9	6	6	31	26	5	5	11	23	49	39
17. Stoke City	42	10	7	4	42	21	3	5	13	16	38	38
18. Birmingham City	42	7	11	3	34	28	3	7	11	24	34	38
19. Portsmouth	42	11	6	4	41	22	2	6	13	21	46	38
20. Grimsby Town	42	11	5	5	29	23	2	7	12	22	45	38
21. Manchester City	42	12	2	7	49	33	2	6	13	31	44	36
22. West Bromwich Albion	42	10	5	6	46	36	4	3	14	28	55	36

Tom Whittaker's side were not short of experience for this campaign. Ronnie Rooke was 36 and the likes of Les Compton and Joe Mercer were not far behind. The seniors guided the Gunners through a fine campaign, which saw them beaten just three times in the first 32 matches. Then, as the volatility of fortune would have it, they lost two out of the next three ties. It all made for plenty of drama. With just five matches to go, Arsenal were nine points clear and needed just a win over Huddersfield to clinch the championship. On the day, they managed just a point, but thanks to results elsewhere it was still enough.

	P	W	D	L	F	A	W	D	L	F	A	Pts
1. Arsenal	**42**	**15**	**3**	**3**	**56**	**15**	**8**	**10**	**3**	**25**	**17**	**59**
2. Manchester United	42	11	7	3	50	27	8	7	6	31	21	52
3. Burnley	42	12	5	4	31	12	8	7	6	25	31	52
4. Derby County	42	11	6	4	38	24	8	6	7	39	33	50
5. Wolverhampton W.	42	12	4	5	45	29	7	5	9	38	41	47
6. Aston Villa	42	13	5	3	42	22	6	4	11	23	35	47
7. Preston North End	42	13	4	4	43	35	7	3	11	24	33	47
8. Portsmouth	42	13	5	3	44	17	6	2	13	24	33	45
9. Blackpool	42	13	4	4	37	14	4	6	11	20	27	44
10. Manchester City	42	13	3	5	37	22	2	9	10	15	25	42
11. Liverpool	42	9	8	4	39	23	7	2	12	26	38	42
12. Sheffield United	42	13	4	4	44	24	3	6	12	21	46	42
13. Charlton Athletic	42	8	4	9	33	29	9	2	10	24	37	40
14. Everton	42	10	2	9	30	26	7	4	10	22	40	40
15. Stoke City	42	9	5	7	29	23	5	5	11	12	32	38
16. Middlesbrough	42	8	7	6	37	27	6	2	13	34	46	37
17. Bolton Wanderers	42	11	2	8	29	25	5	3	13	17	33	37
18. Chelsea	42	11	6	4	38	27	3	3	15	15	44	37
19. Huddersfield Town	42	7	6	8	25	24	5	6	10	26	36	36
20. Sunderland	42	11	4	6	33	18	2	6	13	23	49	36
21. Blackburn Rovers	42	8	5	8	35	30	3	5	13	19	42	32
22. Grimsby Town	42	5	5	11	20	35	3	1	17	25	76	22

1952–53

Here, if ever, was a season for mathematicians. Arsenal and Preston finished with identical records of 21 wins, 12 draws and nine defeats. Therefore, it was necessary to refer to goal average to separate the sides. Here, Whittaker's squad was rewarded for the bold, attacking approach it had taken throughout the season: Arsenal's goal average was 1.516, Preston's was 1.417. The Gunners were therefore crowned champions by the slimmest of margins – 0.099 of a goal. It had not been a vintage campaign in truth. The Gunners finished on 54 points, one of the lowest ever for a title-winning team.

	P	W	D	L	F	A	W	D	L	F	A	Pts
1. Arsenal	**42**	**15**	**3**	**3**	**60**	**30**	**6**	**9**	**6**	**37**	**34**	**54**
2. Preston North End	42	15	3	3	46	25	6	9	6	39	35	54
3. Wolverhampton W.	42	13	5	3	54	27	6	8	7	32	36	51
4. West Bromwich Albion	42	13	3	5	35	19	8	5	8	31	41	50
5. Charlton Athletic	42	12	8	1	47	22	7	3	11	30	41	49
6. Burnley	42	11	6	4	36	20	7	6	8	31	32	48
7. Blackpool	42	13	5	3	45	22	6	4	11	26	48	47
8. Manchester United	42	11	5	5	35	30	7	5	9	34	42	46
9. Sunderland	42	11	9	1	42	27	4	4	13	26	55	43
10. Tottenham Hotspur	42	11	6	4	55	37	4	5	12	23	32	41
11. Aston Villa	42	9	7	5	36	23	5	6	10	27	38	41
12. Cardiff City	42	7	8	6	32	17	7	4	10	22	29	40
13. Middlesbrough	42	12	5	4	46	27	6	13	24	50	39
14. Bolton Wanderers	42	9	4	8	39	35	6	5	10	22	34	39
15. Portsmouth	42	10	6	5	44	34	4	4	13	30	49	38
16. Newcastle United	42	9	5	7	34	33	5	4	12	25	37	37
17. Liverpool	42	10	6	5	36	28	4	2	15	25	54	36
18. Sheffield Wednesday	42	8	6	7	35	32	4	5	12	27	40	35
19. Chelsea	42	10	4	7	35	24	2	7	12	21	42	35
20. Manchester City	42	12	2	7	45	28	2	5	14	27	59	35
21. Stoke City	42	10	4	7	35	26	2	6	13	18	40	34
22. Derby County	42	9	6	6	41	29	2	4	15	18	45	32

1970–71

Bertie Mee's team were awe-inspiring throughout this historic season. They won the league title at White Hart Lane of all places, adding to the delight of fans. Over the season in full it had been a tough 42-match battle to see off the determined fight put up by Leeds United, including during a tough battle at Elland Road. However, the likes of Charlie George, George Graham, Bob Wilson and Frank McLintock stuck to their guns and won the title by a whisker. The scenes of chaotic jubilance that greeted the final whistle at White Hart Lane have rightly entered the Club's folklore.

	P	W	D	L	F	A	W	D	L	F	A	Pts
1. Arsenal	**42**	**18**	**3**	**0**	**41**	**6**	**11**	**4**	**6**	**30**	**23**	**65**
2. Leeds United	42	16	2	3	40	12	11	8	2	32	18	64
3. Tottenham Hotspur	42	11	5	5	33	19	8	9	4	21	14	52
4. Wolverhampton W.	42	13	3	5	33	22	9	5	7	31	32	52
5. Liverpool	42	11	10	0	30	10	6	7	8	12	14	51
6. Chelsea	42	12	6	3	34	21	6	9	6	18	21	51
7. Southampton	42	12	5	4	35	15	5	7	9	21	29	46
8. Manchester United	42	9	6	6	29	24	7	5	9	36	42	43
9. Derby County	42	9	5	7	32	26	7	5	9	24	28	42
10. Coventry City	42	12	4	5	24	12	4	6	11	13	26	42
11. Manchester City	42	7	9	5	30	22	5	8	8	17	20	41
12. Newcastle United	42	9	9	3	27	16	5	4	12	17	30	41
13. Stoke City	42	10	7	4	28	11	2	6	13	16	37	37
14. Everton	42	10	7	4	32	16	2	6	13	22	44	37
15. Huddersfield Town	42	7	8	6	19	16	4	6	11	21	33	36
16. Nottingham Forest	42	9	4	8	29	26	5	4	12	13	35	36
17. West Bromwich Albion	42	9	8	4	34	25	1	7	13	24	50	35
18. Crystal Palace	42	9	5	7	24	24	3	6	12	15	33	35
19. Ipswich Town	42	9	4	8	28	22	3	6	12	14	26	34
20. West Ham United	42	6	8	7	28	30	4	6	11	19	30	34
21. Burnley	42	4	8	9	20	31	3	5	13	9	32	27
22. Blackpool	42	3	9	9	22	31	1	6	14	12	35	23

1988–89

George Graham's first championship as Arsenal Manager will always be remembered for the dramatic end-of-season showdown at Anfield. There, needing to beat the mighty Liverpool by two clear goals, Arsenal did just that, with the second coming in the dying moments from Michael Thomas. Just weeks earlier, the Gunners had nervously dropped home points to Derby County and Wimbledon, leaving the Highbury faithful dejected. The likes of Tony Adams, Paul Merson and Alan Smith had performed like champions for much of the campaign. Away form had been the key, with Arsenal winning 12 away from home compared to just 10 at Highbury.

	P	W	D	L	F	A	W	D	L	F	A	Pts
1. Arsenal	**38**	**10**	**6**	**3**	**35**	**19**	**12**	**4**	**3**	**38**	**17**	**76**
2. Liverpool	38	11	5	3	33	11	11	5	3	32	17	76
3. Nottingham Forest	38	8	7	4	31	16	9	6	4	33	27	64
4. Norwich City	38	8	7	4	23	20	9	4	6	25	25	62
5. Derby County	38	9	3	7	23	18	8	4	7	17	20	58
6. Tottenham Hotspur	38	8	6	5	31	24	7	6	6	29	22	57
7. Coventry City	38	9	4	6	28	23	5	9	5	19	19	55
8. Everton	38	10	7	2	33	18	4	5	10	17	27	54
9. Queens Park Rangers	38	9	5	5	23	16	5	6	8	20	21	53
10. Millwall	38	10	3	6	27	21	4	8	7	20	31	53
11. Manchester United	38	10	5	4	27	13	3	7	9	18	22	51
12. Wimbledon	38	10	3	6	30	19	4	6	9	20	27	51
13. Southampton	38	6	7	6	25	26	4	8	7	27	40	45
14. Charlton Athletic	38	6	7	6	25	24	4	5	10	19	34	42
15. Sheffield Wednesday	38	6	6	7	21	25	4	6	9	13	26	42
16. Luton Town	38	8	6	5	32	21	2	5	12	10	31	41
17. Aston Villa	38	7	6	6	25	22	2	7	10	20	34	40
18. Middlesbrough	38	6	7	6	28	30	3	5	11	16	31	39
19. West Ham United	38	3	6	10	19	30	7	2	10	18	32	38
20. Newcastle United	38	3	6	10	19	28	4	4	11	13	35	31

With David Seaman, Andy Linighan and Anders Limpar added to the squad, the Gunners entered this season rejuvenated and dangerous. They would lose just one league match throughout the campaign, despite some tumultuous dramas on and off the pitch. At one point they trailed Liverpool by eight points after an FA commission deducted Arsenal two points over an incident at Old Trafford. By the time the Gunners took to the field against Manchester United on May bank holiday, they were already champions thanks to Nottingham Forest's defeat of Liverpool earlier that day. A hat-trick from Alan Smith showed that Graham's team were in no mood to let-up.

	P	W	D	L	F	A	W	D	L	F	A	Pts
1. Arsenal	**38**	**15**	**4**	**0**	**51**	**10**	**9**	**9**	**1**	**23**	**8**	**83**
2. Liverpool	38	14	3	2	42	13	9	4	6	35	27	76
3. Crystal Palace	38	11	6	2	26	17	9	3	7	24	24	69
4. Leeds United	38	12	2	5	46	23	7	5	7	19	24	64
5. Manchester City	38	12	3	4	35	25	5	8	6	29	28	62
6. Manchester United	38	11	4	4	34	17	5	8	6	24	28	59
7. Wimbledon	38	8	6	5	28	22	6	8	5	25	24	56
8. Nottingham Forest	38	11	4	4	42	21	3	8	8	23	29	54
9. Everton	38	9	5	5	26	15	4	7	8	24	31	51
10. Tottenham Hotspur	38	8	9	2	35	22	3	7	9	16	28	49
11. Chelsea	38	10	6	3	33	25	3	4	12	25	44	49
12. Queens Park Rangers	38	8	5	6	27	22	4	5	10	17	31	46
13. Sheffield United	38	9	3	7	23	23	4	4	11	13	32	46
14. Southampton	38	9	6	4	33	22	3	3	13	25	47	45
15. Norwich City	38	9	3	7	27	32	4	3	12	14	32	45
16. Coventry City	38	10	6	3	30	16	1	5	13	12	33	44
17. Aston Villa	38	7	9	3	29	25	2	5	12	17	33	41
18. Luton Town	38	7	5	7	22	18	3	2	14	20	43	37
19. Sunderland	38	6	6	7	15	16	2	4	13	23	44	34
20. Derby County	38	3	8	8	25	36	2	1	16	12	39	24

1997–98

In Arsène Wenger's first full season in charge of the Club, Arsenal thrilled their supporters with a league title, their first of the Premiership era. The additions of Marc Overmars, Emmanuel Petit and Nicolas Anelka to a side already including luminaries such as David Seaman, Tony Adams, Patrick Vieira and Dennis Bergkamp proved devastating for the rest of the top-flight. Not only did the Gunners win match after match, they did so in style. Fluent and inventive, the team seemed at times to play on an entirely different level to their opponents. The title was confirmed with a 4–0 victory over Everton at Highbury, a left-footed volley from Tony Adams the pick of the goals.

	P	W	D	L	F	A	W	D	L	F	A	Pts
1. Arsenal	**38**	**15**	**2**	**2**	**43**	**10**	**8**	**7**	**4**	**25**	**23**	**78**
2. Manchester United	38	13	4	2	42	9	10	4	5	31	17	77
3. Liverpool	38	13	2	4	42	16	5	9	5	26	26	65
4. Chelsea	38	13	2	4	37	14	7	1	11	34	29	63
5. Leeds United	38	9	5	5	31	21	8	3	8	26	25	59
6. Blackburn Rovers	38	11	4	4	40	26	5	6	8	17	26	58
7. Aston Villa	38	9	3	7	26	24	8	3	8	23	24	57
8. West Ham United	38	13	4	2	40	18	3	4	12	16	39	56
9. Derby County	38	12	3	4	33	18	4	4	11	19	31	55
10. Leicester City	38	6	13	3	21	15	7	4	8	30	26	53
11. Coventry City	38	8	9	2	26	17	4	7	8	20	27	52
12. Southampton	38	10	1	8	28	23	4	5	10	22	32	48
13. Newcastle United	38	8	5	6	22	20	3	6	10	13	24	44
14. Tottenham Hotspur	38	7	8	4	23	22	4	3	12	21	34	44
15. Wimbledon	38	5	6	8	18	25	5	8	6	16	21	44
16. Sheffield Wednesday	38	9	5	5	30	26	3	3	13	22	41	44
17. Everton	38	7	5	7	25	27	2	8	9	16	29	40
18. Bolton Wanderers	38	7	8	4	25	22	2	5	12	16	39	40
19. Barnsley	38	7	4	8	25	35	3	1	15	12	47	35
20. Crystal Palace	38	2	5	12	15	39	6	4	9	22	32	33

Four years after Wenger's side had won the league (and the double) they repeated the feat. By now, the squad had evolved with fresh attacking talent such as Freddie Ljungberg and Thierry Henry. The team's fluid, quick-passing game, resulted in them scoring in every single league game en route to the title. Nonetheless, it had proved a closely fought league season, with Liverpool joining Manchester United as challengers. Winning their last 13 league fixtures gave Arsenal the edge, and the title-clinching match came at Old Trafford. They needed just a point to guarantee the championship but went one better when Sylvain Wiltord scored the game's only goal.

	P	W	D	L	F	A	W	D	L	F	A	Pts
1. Arsenal	**38**	**12**	**4**	**3**	**42**	**25**	**14**	**5**	**0**	**37**	**11**	**87**
2. Liverpool	38	12	5	2	33	14	12	3	4	34	16	80
3. Manchester United	38	11	2	6	40	17	13	3	3	47	28	77
4. Newcastle United	38	12	3	4	40	23	9	5	5	34	29	71
5. Leeds United	38	9	6	4	31	21	9	6	4	22	16	66
6. Chelsea	38	11	4	4	43	21	6	9	4	23	17	64
7. West Ham United	38	12	4	3	32	14	3	4	12	16	43	53
8. Aston Villa	38	8	7	4	22	17	4	7	8	24	30	50
9. Tottenham Hotspur	38	10	4	5	32	24	4	4	11	17	29	50
10. Blackburn Rovers	38	8	6	5	33	20	4	4	11	22	31	46
11. Southampton	38	7	5	7	23	22	5	4	10	23	32	45
12. Middlesbrough	38	7	5	7	23	26	5	4	10	12	21	45
13. Fulham	38	7	7	5	21	16	3	7	9	15	28	44
14. Charlton Athletic	38	5	6	8	23	30	5	8	6	15	19	44
15. Everton	38	8	4	7	26	23	3	6	10	19	34	43
16. Bolton Wanderers	38	5	7	7	20	31	4	6	9	24	31	40
17. Sunderland	38	7	7	5	18	16	3	3	13	11	35	40
18. Ipswich Town	38	6	4	9	20	24	3	5	11	21	40	36
19. Derby County	38	5	4	10	20	26	3	2	14	13	37	30
20. Leicester City	38	3	7	9	15	34	2	6	11	15	30	28

2003–04

After four straight wins at the start of this league season, the Gunners almost lost at Old Trafford but were saved when Ruud van Nistelrooy's late penalty smashed off the crossbar. The visitors emerged with their unbeaten record intact – and it remained that way for the entire league season. What a season it was: Arsenal recorded some iconic victories at Elland Road, Stamford Bridge and Anfield, and scored a plethora of wonder goals, including a fine winner at Liverpool in October. In April, when Liverpool visited Highbury, the team showed true character when they overcame a 2–1 half-time deficit to win 4–2 and stay on course for the title.

	P	W	D	L	F	A	W	D	L	F	A	Pts
1. Arsenal	**38**	**15**	**4**	**0**	**40**	**14**	**11**	**8**	**0**	**33**	**12**	**90**
2. Chelsea	38	12	4	3	34	13	12	3	4	33	17	79
3. Manchester United	38	12	4	3	37	15	11	2	6	27	20	75
4. Liverpool	38	10	4	5	29	15	6	8	5	26	22	60
5. Newcastle United	38	11	5	3	33	14	2	12	5	19	26	56
6. Aston Villa	38	9	6	4	24	19	6	5	8	24	25	56
7. Charlton Athletic	38	7	6	6	29	29	7	5	7	22	22	53
8. Bolton Wanderers	38	6	8	5	24	21	8	3	8	24	35	53
9. Fulham	38	9	4	6	29	21	5	6	8	23	25	52
10. Birmingham City	38	8	5	6	26	24	4	9	6	17	24	50
11. Middlesbrough	38	8	4	7	25	23	5	5	9	19	29	48
12. Southampton	38	8	6	5	24	17	4	5	10	20	28	47
13 Portsmouth	38	10	4	5	35	19	2	5	12	12	35	45
14. Tottenham Hotspur	38	9	4	6	33	27	4	2	13	14	30	45
15. Blackburn Rovers	38	5	4	10	25	31	7	4	8	26	28	44
16. Manchester City	38	5	9	5	31	24	4	5	10	24	30	41
17. Everton	38	8	5	6	27	20	1	7	11	18	37	39
18. Leicester City	38	3	10	6	19	28	3	5	11	29	37	33
19. Leeds United	38	5	7	7	25	31	3	2	14	15	48	33
20. Wolverhampton W.	38	7	5	7	23	35	0	7	12	15	42	33

Roll of Honour

League Champions (13 times)
1931 1933 1934 1935 1938 1948 1953 1971 1989 1991
1998 2002 2004
(runners-up 1926 1932 1973 1999 2000 2001 2003 2005)

FA Cup (10)
1930 1936 1950 1971 1979 1993 1998 2002 2003 2005
(runners-up 1927 1932 1952 1972 1978 1980 2001)

League Cup (2)
1987 1993
(runners-up 1968 1969 1988 2011)

UEFA Champions League
runners-up 2006

UEFA Cup
1970
(runners-up 2000)

European Cup Winners' Cup
1994
(runners-up 1980 1995)

CHAPTER 4

Arsenal Legends

Throughout the Club's illustrious history, a special class of player has been among those to pull on the famous red and white shirt of Arsenal. These are those competitors who make contributions of such significance and quality that their stature soars towards talismanic heights. Some are recent heroes, while others are from many decades back. Each richly deserves their place in this chapter, which will delight Gunners fans.

Readers will have their own opinions on which players should have been chosen to fill this chapter. Arsenal's history is so rich with legendary players that one could fill a book with such names. Nevertheless, these potted biographies recall the qualities that made the players so special and describe their many achievements for Arsenal. With a complimentary box of career statistics and a trivia fact for each player, here is all you need to know about the legends of Arsenal's history.

In this chapter, we will profile players from throughout the Club's history and in every position. From goalkeeping legend David Seaman, to stalwart defenders such as Tony Adams and Frank McLintock. Also profiled are midfielders from down the ages including Irishman Liam Brady and French star Patrick Vieira. Strikers including Cliff Bastin, Ian Wright and Dennis Bergkamp are also among those chronicled.

Tony Adams

Even if you were to lay down on a table the many medals that Tony Adams won during his illustrious 18-year Gunners career, they would only begin to tell the story of his place in Arsenal history. A colossus of a captain, he contributed an incalculable amount to the Gunners cause and was the quintessential one-club man.

He made his debut in 1983, just weeks after his 17th birthday. It was a rarity: a poor Adams performance, in which he was partly to blame for one of the goals in a 2–1 defeat. Yet under the subsequent reign of George Graham, Adams blossomed into one of the finest centre-halves in English footballing history. The towering defender was named PFA Young Player of the Year in Graham's first season at the helm and was named captain in the following campaign.

In 1989, Adams led the Club to its famous league title, grabbed at the last minute at fortress Anfield. Two years later he again lifted the league trophy, yet by now Adams was a controversial figure. He had been jailed in 1991 and had also faced cruel "donkey" taunts from opposition fans. Typically, he used these setbacks as motivation to do better.

During the latter years of Graham's reign, the Gunners found success in the knockout competitions both domestically and in Europe. Adams was magnificent, keeping things tighter than ever at the back and chipping in with key goals against, among others, Tottenham, Ipswich Town and Torino. His aerial dominance, crunching tackles and organisational prowess were all underpinned by his trademarks: fearlessness and utter commitment.

When Arsène Wenger took over, some commentators predicted that Adams, by now in his thirties, might be shown the door. Instead, he underwent something of a renaissance under the Frenchman. His defending remained as solid as ever, but was joined by a new confidence and flair. Typical of this were his stunning left-footed volleyed goals against Tottenham Hotspur and Everton, the latter crowning the match that saw Arsenal win its first Premiership trophy.

In his final season, Adams led Wenger's team to one more league title. This meant he became the first Arsenal player to win league titles in three separate decades and the first Gunner to captain the Club to two doubles. He left on a high, having won 10 major trophies for Arsenal. Will such iconic commitment and service ever be repeated in the future?

DID YOU KNOW THAT?
In the late 1990s, Tony Adams learned French and took piano playing lessons.

For the Record

Born: 10 October 1966, Romford, Essex
Country: England, 66 appearances, 5 goals
Arsenal appearances: 669
Arsenal goals: 48
Arsenal debut: H v Sunderland, 5 November
   1983, League

Cliff Bastin

Back in 1929, when Herbert Chapman splashed out the-then considerable fee of £2,000 on a 17-year-old Exeter City player who had turned out just 17 times for the Devonian side, it hardly seemed he had pulled off a game-changing transfer coup. Yet that is exactly what Chapman had done – for he had secured the services of the man who would set and then hold the Club's goalscoring record for six decades.

The teenager broke through quickly. At the end of his first season with the Gunners, Bastin had an FA Cup winners' medal under his belt. Yet the best was still to come for him. By the time he turned 19, young Bastin had also won a league title and an England cap. He was the youngest player to achieve that particular hat-trick. In total he earned five league titles with Arsenal and added a second FA Cup triumph in 1936.

Bastin's goals had powered all of those triumphs. His goalscoring prowess is all the more impressive when you recall that he played not as a striker, but an outside-left. Unlike some wingers who hugged the touchline, Cliff was content to stand further infield, ready to exploit any opportunity that came his way. Indeed, he would regularly cut inside and run onto one of Alex James's incisive passes.

Such moves would often finish in a goal to the delight of Arsenal fans, whose question marks over Bastin had long since evaporated. In fact, Bastin's role as a goalscorer rather than provider was innovative for an outside-left. Not for the first, nor last, time, Chapman's tactics would prove to be original and influential.

When Ted Drake arrived in 1934, Bastin's role became as much about creating as scoring goals. His versatility proved priceless, not least because assist-king Alex James fell injured. However, even while pulling the strings for Drake, Bastin still scored 17 goals during the 1935–36 and 1936–37 campaigns. You can't keep a good goalscorer down, after all.

A combination of injuries and the Second World War cut Bastin's playing days off in their prime. Yet his total of 178 goals was enough to make him the Club's leading goalscorer. His record would stand until the late 1990s, when a certain Ian Wright surpassed it, before Thierry Henry then outgunned Wright. Cliff Bastin died on 4 December 1991. The fact he is still widely and regularly discussed in the 21st century, nearly 100 years after his playing days, shows just what a shrewd signing he was by Chapman.

DID YOU KNOW THAT?
Cliff Bastin suffered from deafness during his playing days.

For the Record
Born: 14 March 1912, Exeter, Devon
Country: England, 21 appearances, 12 goals
Arsenal appearances: 396
Arsenal goals: 178
Arsenal debut: A v Everton, 5 October 1929,
   League

Dennis Bergkamp

Dennis Bergkamp's arrival at Arsenal in 1995 provoked a number of strong emotions: Arsenal fans could hardly believe the Club had landed such a magical talent, while some sceptics predicted the Dutchman's stay would be brief and disappointing. Eleven years, three league championships, four FA cups and countless moments of magic later, he retired in glory. His achievements for Arsenal had, if anything, exceeded the wildest of expectations.

Bergkamp, who started his career with Ajax where he scored 75 goals in 91 games, arrived in London following a disappointing spell in Italy. While his magical abilities were rarely doubted, he had lost form and confidence in Serie A. However, in the English league he quickly found his feet. He built a strong rapport with fellow striker Ian Wright in his first campaign, helping to propel the team to European qualification. Then, Arsène Wenger arrived and Dennis, like so many Gunners of the day, never looked back.

Wenger would later describe the Dutchman's presence in the squad he inherited as "a blessing, a gift when I arrived". For here was a player whose poise, grace and class dovetailed beautifully with the Frenchman's vision. In Wenger's first full season with the Club, Bergkamp enjoyed a vintage campaign, his goals and passes the majestic basis of the Double triumph. He won the PFA and Football Writers' Player of the Year awards and took first, second and third places in the BBC's Goal of the Month competition following his stunning hat-trick against Leicester City.

It speaks volumes for the fortunes of both Club and player that it was not until the 2001–02 season that

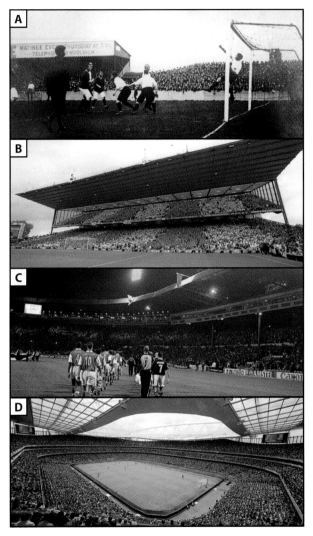

PICTURE QUIZ 1: Gatherings of the Arsenal faithful
Can you identify these "home" venues for the Gunners?

PICTURE QUIZ 2: Simply Hair-Raising

Arsenal players of recent times have sometimes perturbed onlookers with their statement hairstyles. Can you name this barbershop quartet?

PICTURE QUIZ 3: Celebrate Good Times

Can you name these Arsenal legends and what was their particular cause for celebration?

PICTURE QUIZ 4: The Road to Rio

The following Arsenal players all took part in the 2014 FIFA World Cup qualifying campaign. Who are they? And name the countries for which they were battling to clinch a place in the Finals.

PICTURE QUIZ 5: Remind You of Anybody?

Arsenal supporters have been highly inventive when it comes to player nicknames. What's the monicker and who's the player in each case?

PICTURE QUIZ 6: Meet the Gaffer

These four happy fellas went on to be the manager of the Arsenal. Can you name them?

PICTURE QUIZ 7: They Shall Not Pass

Arsenal have had many fine goalkeepers down the years. Who are these four esteemed custodians? And pick out the Englishman, the Scotsman, the Welshman and the Irishman.

PICTURE QUIZ 8: New Kid on the Block

Who were these big-name signings for the Gunners, and where did they hail from?

ANSWERS ON PAGE 160

the Dutchman again reached such heights – and that when he did so the Gunners won another Double. As he approached his mid-thirties he remained breathtaking. His wonder goal at St James Park was rivalled by assists for a series of match-winners from Freddie Ljungberg, as the team sauntered to glory once more.

The unbeaten run which saw the Club win the 2004 league title saw a twilight-era Bergkamp again influential. By now, his authority was as strong off the pitch as on it: the younger members of the squad naturally looked up to this footballing legend and he was only too happy to lend his wisdom and support to them, hinting at a future in coaching. Even as he retired, there was something special about Dennis. In the final season at Highbury, there was a "Dennis Bergkamp Day", in which he scored against West Bromwich Albion, and then his testimonial kicked-off the Emirates Stadium era.

DID YOU KNOW THAT?
Dennis Bergkamp often travelled by car or train to far-flung away matches, due to a fear of flying.

For the Record
Born: 10 May 1969, Amsterdam, Holland
Country: Netherlands, 79 appearances, 37 goals
Arsenal appearances: 423
Arsenal goals: 120
Arsenal debut: H v Middlesbrough, 20 August
   1995, League

Liam Brady

During his earliest years with Arsenal after signing schoolboy forms in 1970, Liam Brady was written off by several observers. Slender and of average height, it was feared that the tender Irishman would be swallowed whole by the monster that was 1970s English football. While such concerns were understandable to an extent, the slight Dubliner would quickly prove that brain can outwit brawn.

Hailing from a footballing family, Liam was a true midfield maestro. His grace was typified by his remarkable left foot, which conjured many a goal and assist for the Gunners. His vision, footballing brain and speed of thought outwitted opponents, right from his 1973 debut at the age of 17. By the start of the following season he had earned himself a central place in Bertie Mee's side alongside George Armstrong and England World Cup winner Alan Ball. He was bold, nimble and highly creative. After Ball left for Southampton in 1976, Brady took centre stage and guided the Club to three successive FA Cup finals.

The first Wembley final was against Ipswich Town. The Irishman was in uncharacteristically subdued mood on the day and the Gunners lost 1–0. The following year, they faced Manchester United. This time, Arsenal won and nobody was more influential under the twin towers than Brady. After United had drawn level at 2–2 in the closing minutes of the tie, Brady lifted his head and surged upfield with the ball. He then released a perfect pass for Alan Sunderland to score the iconic winner.

The following campaign was his final season for Arsenal. He opened the season with a goal in a 4–0 win against Brighton. In the FA Cup campaign, he was once again highly influential in the Club's road to Wembley. He was present in all four of the epic semi-finals against Liverpool but could not overcome West Ham United's defensive tactics in the final. He had experienced more joy in the semi-final of the European Cup-Winners' Cup against Juventus, the team he would leave Arsenal for in the summer of 1980.

After a glorious time in Italy, Brady returned to England where he joined West Ham United and later managed Celtic. He finally returned to Arsenal to take up the role of head of youth development in 1996. Under the Irishman, the Club has enjoyed a string of wins in youth tournaments and the first team has featured many a graduate of his tutelage. Although he will leave the Club in 2014, Brady's influence will live on.

DID YOU KNOW THAT?
Liam Brady won the league title twice during his two years with Juventus.

For the Record
Born: 13 February 1956, Dublin, Ireland
Country: Republic of Ireland, 72 appearances,
    9 goals
Arsenal appearances: 307
Arsenal goals: 59
Arsenal debut: H v Birmingham City, 6 October
    1973, League

Ted Drake

He was an imposing goal machine who scored an astonishing 42 league goals in the title-winning season of 1934–35. He was the top scorer for each of the five full seasons he spent with the Club. A former gas inspector, Edward Joseph Drake proved to be an explosive centre-forward and certainly put the wind up his opponents. He was a powerful, strong and courageous player. His example richly vindicated the saying that fortune favours the brave.

Born in Southampton, Drake spent three seasons with his hometown club, during which he quickly built a reputation as a fine goalscorer. He scored 47 goals in 71 appearances for the Saints before George Allison snapped him up and took him to north London. He scored on his league debut, which came against Wolves on 24 March 1934. He had joined too late to qualify for a league-winners' medal, but he would make up for that the following year.

Drake's goals were at the heart of the Gunners' title charge of 1934–35. His historic league haul included three hat-tricks and four four-goal hauls. He also scored in the FA Cup and Charity Shield. Who could have thought that he would surpass that achievement the following year? Yet in the eyes of many that is exactly what Drake would do.

Perhaps his most spectacular achievement came against Aston Villa during the 1935–36 season. Arsenal walloped their opponents 7–1 – and each Gunners goal was scored by Drake. In fact, only the crossbar prevented him from scoring eight on the day. (Curiously, Drake's record for the most goals scored in one game stood for just 12 days as Bunny Bell of Tranmere scored nine against Oldham in the Third Division North.)

In total, Drake scored 139 goals in 184 games for Arsenal. His lethal form earned him England call-ups aplenty, and he appeared in the "Battle of Highbury" against Italy in November 1934. Naturally, he scored the winner in a bitterly fought 3–2 win. He also represented his country militarily, serving for the RAF during the First World War.

When Drake turned to management he once more made history. Following promising spells with Hendon and Reading, he took over the reins at Chelsea. There, in the 1954–55 season, he guided the Blues to the First Division championship. It would be their only top-flight title of the twentieth century, and Drake became the first player to win the Championship as a player and as a manager.

Ted Drake died in May 1995, aged 82. His legacy lives on and stands as an example to any youngster looking to make a name for themselves in a game. It's a special player who can score all seven goals in a 7–1 victory, after all.

DID YOU KNOW THAT?
Ted Drake also played cricket, representing Hampshire CCC.

For the Record
Born: 16 August 1912, Southampton, Hampshire
Country: England, 5 appearances, 6 goals
Arsenal appearances: 184
Arsenal goals: 139
Arsenal debut: H v Wolverhampton Wanderers,
    24 March 1934, League

Cesc Fabregas

League cup ties against Rotherham United are not normally expected to become historic occasions for Arsenal. Yet when a young, slight Spanish teenager came on as a substitute in such a tie in 2003, it not only marked the Club's youngest-ever first-team debutant, it also heralded the beginning of a legendary Gunners career.

Cesc Fabregas hinted at his magnificence from the earliest days of his Arsenal career. In his first full season for the Club, the 2004–05 campaign, he showed energy, poise and technique which belied his tender years. Learning from the towering Patrick Vieira, Cesc bossed the midfield and dictated the very rhythm of the games. An FA Cup winners' medal was suitable reward for his endeavours, yet the best was still to come.

The following campaign, Cesc found himself with renewed responsibility following the departure of Vieira. The diminutive teenager revelled in his new status and soared. When Vieira returned with Juventus in the Champions League, Cesc outclassed his former midfield partner and struck a richly symbolic opening goal to confirm his brilliance. The following year he provided 13 assists, as his labours in the middle of the park were increasingly joined by dazzling creativity further forward. He was named in Uefa's 2006 Team of the Year and was nominated for the PFA Player of the Year and Young Player of the Year awards.

In 2008 he blossomed further. During 12 glorious months the Spaniard was named Gunners captain, crowned as the PFA Young Player of the Year, and became a European champion with Spain. As Wenger awarded him a more attacking position, in a single season he scored 15 goals and created the same number. On the international stage he continued to thrive, providing a pass that set up Spain's 2010 World Cup final winner.

In August 2011, he left the Club to rejoin his boyhood heroes of Barcelona. It was an emotional parting of the ways, not least for Cesc when he bid Wenger farewell. "I spoke to him to say goodbye and got very emotional because he has been like a father figure," he said. Speaking of Arsenal, he added: "I went from being a boy to a man and they gave me absolutely everything in football." Gunners fans had loved watching his transition.

Since leaving the Club, Cesc has continued to develop. He has played in an advanced role for Barcelona and Spain. He also continues to pay tribute to Arsenal Football Club, where he honed his talent. It goes to show what debuts against Rotherham United can lead to.

DID YOU KNOW THAT?

Cesc once presented his own television programme, which was inspirationally called *The Cesc Fabregas Show*.

For the Record

Born: 4 May 1987, Arenys de Mar, Spain

Country: Spain, 81 appearances, 13 goals

Arsenal appearances: 303

Arsenal goals: 57

Arsenal debut: H v Rotherham United, 28 October 2003, League Cup

---

George Graham

The contrast between George Graham's style as an Arsenal player and an Arsenal manager was stark, to say the least. During the 1960s and 70s, he was known as "Stroller", thanks to his languid style of play. As manager in the 1980s and 90s, he was a disciplinarian who valued nothing more than rigid play and hard-working commitment. Put a different way, it is unlikely that Graham the manager would have been keen to manage Graham the player.

The crowning glory of his playing years came in the 1970–71 season. He was a pivotal star of the double-winning Gunners side, even claiming a goal in the FA Cup final victory over Liverpool. As the Arsenal faithful had celebrated the league title that year, little could they know it would be the Club's last until 1989, and that the manager at the helm for that win would be Graham.

When he was appointed Arsenal manager in 1986, he had only previously been boss at Millwall. The Club had been treading water for some time and were in urgent need of a decisive, fearless manager. They got just that, with Graham revitalising the Club. At the heart of the Graham revolution was his successful promotion of a series of young, homegrown players such as David Rocastle, Tony Adams and Michael Thomas. Thanks to some shrewd purchases, including defenders Nigel Winterburn and Steve Bould, he was quickly winning matches and then trophies – the first of which came in the shape of the 1987 League Cup.

Yet it was the 1989 league championship which most will still see as the Scot's finest hour. Graham's confidence and tactical nous was pivotal throughout the campaign, never less so than during the decisive showdown at Anfield on 26 May 1989. Two years later, Arsenal were champions again, this time winning the title by seven points, losing just one game while conceding only 18 goals.

Graham had by the end of 1991 made several significant purchases, including those of David Seaman, Alan Smith and Ian Wright. During the latter years of his managerial reign the Gunners became knockout kings, winning the FA Cup, League Cup and European Cup-Winners' Cup over 12 magnificent months. His side had, accordingly, become more solid and defensive than his previous charges. He took the criticism on the chin.

The legacy of Graham, who left the Club in 1995, is unquestionable. He plucked Arsenal from mid-table mediocrity and guided them to their greatest period of success since the 1930s. Several of his players, including Tony Adams and Martin Keown, continued to star for the Club deep into Wenger's reign.

DID YOU KNOW THAT?

After leaving Arsenal, George Graham managed Leeds United and, controversially, Tottenham Hotspur.

For the Record

Born: 30 November 1944, Glasgow, Scotland

Country: Scotland, 12 appearances, 3 goals

Arsenal appearances: 308

Arsenal goals: 77

Arsenal debut: H v Leicester City, 1 October 1966, League

Thierry Henry

When Henry arrived at Highbury, he had a lot to prove. His career had rather lost its way at Juventus, and as a Gunner he would be moved from his familiar terrain of the left-wing, into a central striking role. Not for the first, nor the last, time, plenty of people doubted the wisdom of Wenger's move – and yet again the manager was vindicated when his plan paid off beautifully. Henry is the Club's all-time greatest goalscorer, who won two league championships, two FA Cups and millions of admirers across the globe.

Henry's combination of grace, pace and skill made for a mesmeric sight. When he soared towards goal with the ball at his feet he made for an almost balletic figure. He brought defenders to their knees and was the bane of goalkeepers' existences, such was his deadly pace and clinical finishing. His goals, which were rarely ordinary, shot the team all the way to the 2001–02 Double. His confidence and swagger only added to the thrill of the spectacle he conjured. As Bob Wilson put it: "He's like a Rolls-Royce when he goes past people."

After the departure of Patrick Vieira, Henry was handed the captain's armband. His influence on the players around him had for sometime been clear. Indeed, as well as scoring, he often created goals for others. For instance, during the 2003–04 campaign he had added to the 30 goals he scored with assists for 20 other strikes. He would win the Player of the Year award five times as a Gunner and twice came second in the FIFA World Player of the Year ranking.

"He's a fantastic striker – the exception becomes

the norm with him," said Wenger of his captain as he continued to torment opponents. Indeed, before a ball was kicked the mere presence of the deadly Frenchman had inflicted a blow into the hearts of many rivals. How would they control the conjurer? Towards the end of his Arsenal career, Henry was troubled by injuries. Yet when he left for Barcelona in the summer of 2007, there was not a Gunners fan who did not appreciate all he had done for the Club.

Yet, as was so often the case with the unpredictable Henry, there was one more twist left in the tale. While a New York Red Bulls player in 2011, he returned to Arsenal for a two-month loan spell. Showing humility, the returning hero said: "I'll be on the bench most of the time – if I can make the bench, that is." The now bearded-one duly scored against Leeds United. It was a trademark goal that reminded Arsenal what a performer he had always been.

DID YOU KNOW THAT?
Time magazine featured Thierry Henry in its 2007 list of the world's most 100 influential people.

For the Record
Born: 17 August 1977, Paris, France
Country: France, 123 appearances, 51 goals
Arsenal appearances: 377
Arsenal goals: 228
Arsenal debut: H v Leicester City, 7 August 1999, League

Frank McLintock

Born in Glasgow and raised in the city's uncompromising Gorbals district, Frank McLintock's first English club was Leicester City. His stamina and level of contribution were both strong. His endeavours in the middle of the park helped the Foxes to the FA Cup final in 1961 and 1963. His side were runners-up in both, heightening the Scot's hunger for silverware. Further, the cup runs had helped bring him to the attention of Billy Wright, who brought McLintock, by now 24, to Highbury.

His energy, work-rate and commitment enormously enhanced a Gunners side which had been struggling for consistency. He quickly showed that as well as his concrete footballing prowess, he also had a strong leadership role. His head would never drop and in the heat of the battle he set a fine example for his team-mates. He would reach two League Cup finals and once more he would be on the losing side, this time against Leeds United in 1968 and Swindon Town in 1969.

During the 1970s, the Scot played in defence. Having been moved back there during an injury crisis, he made such a success of life at the back that he remained there. Playing alongside Peter Simpson, the Scot added extra bite to an already solid unit and thus helped form a solid Gunners rearguard. By now captain, McLintock was proving to be an inspiring leader for the team in good times and bad. During the following season, he would lead the team to the best of times.

Frank missed just one of the Club's 64 games during the 1970–71 season by the end of which Arsenal had won their first Double. As the pressure built during the run-in, he only grew in poise and stature – even scoring three times during high-pressure ties in April. When the title was won at White Hart Lane, the Scottish skipper was chaired off the pitch by his team-mates, such was the esteem they held him in. However, for Frank there was an added personal dimension to the season's next and final hurdle.

Having been on the losing side four times in Cup finals, he was determined to lift a cup this time. He was at his commanding best as Arsenal beat Liverpool under the Twin Towers in the FA Cup. As Charlie George, the hero at Wembley as the Gunners beat Liverpool, said of the captain, "[He was] always there, always encouraging, and cajoling when necessary, he got the last drop of blood out of every Arsenal player who wore the shirt beside him." He was named Footballer of the Year for the campaign.

Later, he played for Queens Park Rangers, before managing Leicester City and Brentford. He is now a respected pundit where his robust and wise views recall some of the greatest qualities he showed as a player.

DID YOU KNOW THAT?
Frank McLintock was awarded an MBE in 1972.

For the Record
Born: 28 December 1939, Glasgow, Scotland
Country: Scotland, 9 appearances, 1 goal
Arsenal appearances: 403
Arsenal goals: 32
Arsenal debut: H v Nottingham Forest,
   6 October 1964, League

David Seaman

When manager George Graham consulted with Gunners goalkeeping legend Bob Wilson over his proposed purchase of David Seaman in 1990, Wilson was adamant that he should sign the QPR stopper. "You're not even taking a risk," Wilson told him – and how right he was. In the season prior to Seaman's arrival, Arsenal lost 12 games and conceded 38 goals; in his first campaign between the sticks, the Gunners lost one game and conceded just 18 goals.

Goalkeepers are rarely lauded for their entertainment value, yet Seaman was pure box office. Many of his saves are as fondly recalled by Gunners fans as the goals of star strikers. The breathtaking reach of his save from Paul Peschisolido in an FA Cup semi-final against Sheffield United and the Yorkshireman's penalty shoot-out heroics in the semi-final of the European Cup-Winners' Cup against Sampdoria linger fondly in the memory.

He had hit the ground running with a league championship medal in his first season as a Gunner. To their frustration, opponents found he was the complete custodian: a quick-thinking shot-stopping, cross-catching diamond. His distribution was also on the money, and he claimed several assists for goals at the other end. As Arsenal became the first English club to win the FA and League cups in one season, it was to the goalkeeper they could look for a large slice of the credit.

When the Club reached two successive European Cup-Winners' Cup finals, winning the first one, Seaman was largely peerless. "1–0 to the Arsenal," became the fans' anthem, and it was he, as much as anyone, who was responsible for the "nil" in that song. Against Parma in the 1994 final, he played with a rib injury to help the team to victory. Throughout the following campaign, Seaman was just as influential, though Nayim intervened cruelly at the death in Paris.

Arsène Wenger noted with approval how, the older Seaman got, the harder he trained, so determined was he to improve and prolong his career. The sweat paid off, Seaman played deep into his thirties and was between the sticks for the 1998 and 2002 double-winning campaigns. Even many neutrals were pleased for him – his heroics for England during Euro 96 and his affable personality had won him many fans.

An intelligent, committed and gifted player, Seaman was an example to all who followed his fortunes. All players have their critics. Yet no one was a fiercer critic of the Yorkshireman than Seaman himself. Such was his quest for perfection that he put his every move on the pitch under the microscope. That is the way of the winner.

DID YOU KNOW THAT?
David Seaman's nicknames included "H" (amongst the players) and "Safe Hands".

For the Record
Born: 19 September 1963, Rotherham, Yorkshire
Country: England, 75 caps
Arsenal appearances: 564
Arsenal debut: H v Wimbledon, 25 August 1990,
    League

Patrick Vieira

During his eight years with the Club, Patrick Vieira was, in every sense, at the heart of the team. On the field, he patrolled the central pastures with authority, poise and flair. That authority followed him off the field, too. He became a fans' favourite within minutes of his first appearance in red and white, and remained so throughout his Arsenal tenure.

The Frenchman began his career in north London as something of an ambassador. As Arsène Wenger's first signing, he arrived before the new manager officially took over. Coming on as a substitute against Sheffield Wednesday for his debut, he instantly transformed the match. In doing so he gave a glowing, and accurate, indicator of what joys lay ahead under Wenger.

Quickly, Vieira's enormous and well-rounded talents became legendary in English football. The athletic, Senegal-born midfielder was an influential presence, dictating the tempo of the game throughout the field. He won the ball powerfully, dribbled with graceful pace, and passed with deadly accuracy. By the end of his first season in England, he was already a hugely respected force.

Yet, if anything, the best was yet to come. Throughout the 1997–98 season, his imperious and tireless endeavour was crucial to the Club's double-winning campaign. He added goalscoring to his already bountiful repertoire, with a crashing volley against Newcastle United a particularly memorable strike. He was just as influential in the 2001–2002 double-winning campaign.

He was the natural and successful successor as captain when Tony Adams hung up his boots. With the captain's armband he carried himself with yet more authority, the disciplinary problems that dogged his early years were largely consigned to the past. Few players could have succeeded such a colossus as Adams so confidently.

Vieira's finest achievement for the Club was leading the Gunners through a 49-match unbeaten run. He opened the scoring at White Hart Lane on the day the "Invincibles" won the 2004 league title. This capped an extraordinary season for both Club and captain. The following season, he won the FA Cup for Arsenal with his last kick for the Club. His spot-kick in the Cardiff shoot-out proved to be the decisive one. From start to finish of his Gunners career, he had been talismanic.

With Vieira remaining in the game after his playing career, the prospect of a new chapter in his Arsenal story remains tantalisingly possible.

DID YOU KNOW THAT?

Patrick Vieira appeared for both Milan giants. He played for AC Milan in 1996 and turned out for Internazionale between 2006 and 2010.

For the Record
Born: 23 June 1976, Dakar, Senegal
Country: France, 107 appearances, 6 goals
Arsenal appearances: 406
Arsenal goals: 33
Arsenal debut: H v Sheffield Wednesday,
    16 September 1996, League

Ian Wright

When George Graham brought Ian Wright to Highbury in 1991, some questioned the wisdom of the move. At the time, the Gunners boasted the striking prowess of Alan Smith, Kevin Campbell and Paul Merson, with the promising Andy Cole on the fringes of the first-team squad. For Wright, the scepticism merely offered him another chance to prove people wrong – something he'd been doing since the first time he kicked a football.

After a series of setbacks and rejections, Wright only broke into the professional game at the age of 21. He suffered two broken legs while with Crystal Palace but overcame both to continue making his name as a top striker, thus coming under the watchful eye of Graham. Once a Gunner, Wright became a leading light for the Club with the sort of speed and determination that terrified opposition defenders.

He scored four goals in his first two games for Arsenal and went on to net 14 in his first 12 matches. His confidence and speed were astonishing; he outfoxed opposition with panache and effervescence. The Highbury faithful could hardly believe their luck as Wright became the fastest player at that stage to reach 100 goals for the Club, overturning a record that had belonged to Ted Drake for 40 years.

Subsequently, Wright became the Club's leading goalscorer, bettering Cliff Bastin's 178-strong tally with a hat-trick against Bolton in 1997. So many of his strikes had been wonder goals, his finishing as imaginative as it was impeccable. During a career in which Wright in turns dazzled, delighted and dumbfounded, he won a clean sweep of domestic honours in an Arsenal shirt: one league title, an FA Cup and League Cup.

Due to a combination of injuries and the emergence of Nicolas Anelka, Wright's final year with the Club saw him make only limited appearances. Yet he bowed out as a significant contributor to the double-winning side of 1998. In 2000, he was awarded the MBE for services to football by Her Majesty The Queen. He described it as "the most humbling and nerve-wracking experience of my life".

Wright's bubbly, enthusiastic persona was a source of inspiration to all who played alongside him. Some of his goal celebrations were as delightfully memorable as the strikes themselves. His records were subsequently broken by Thierry Henry, and the Frenchman has often acknowledged the debt he owes his predecessor for the example he set him. That's a measure of a great: a player whose influence lives on long after he has left the scene.

DID YOU KNOW THAT?

Ian Wright scored a total of 305 goals in his entire football career.

For the Record

Born: 3 November 1963, London

Country: England, 33 appearances, 9 goals

Arsenal appearances: 288

Arsenal goals: 185

Arsenal debut: A v Leicester City, 8 October
    1991, League Cup

CHAPTER 5

Gunners Arsenal
nal Gunners A
Gunners Arsenal
nal Gunners A

Arsenal Fantasy Teams

It is the favourite pastime of many an Arsenal fan: to assemble a fantasy line-up of your favourite football club. Sometimes this is as simple an all-time Gunners eleven, or sometimes you might employ a more creative, or even left-field, criteria, as you step into an imaginary manager's position.

In chapter five you will find eight Gunners dream teams, assembled for your reading pleasure. From the ultimate English line-ups from three different eras to all-time Irish, Northern Irish and Scottish teams.

You will also find two ultimate elevens comprised of players from other European nations, and a cracking line-up of Gunners stars who have won, or made a major impact at, international tournaments. Although these stars come from different eras of the Club's history, they make for a mouth-watering combination in one's mind: imagine Alan Ball rolling the ball from midfield for Kanu to set-up George Eastham!

Why not assemble some fantasy teams of your own? You can either use the same headings as here but include your choices, or come up with some themes of your own. Of course, if you want a really red-hot Arsenal discussion, you could gather some fellow Gooners and see if you can agree on an ultimate Arsenal eleven. Happy choosing!

English Football League XI (1880s–1960s)

1
George
SWINDIN

2
Tom
PARKER

4
Peter
STOREY

5
Eddie
HAPGOOD

3
Percy
SANDS

7
George
ARMSTRONG

6
Alex
JAMES

8
Denis
COMPTON

11
Ray
BOWDEN

9
Ted
DRAKE

10
Cliff
BASTIN

DID YOU KNOW THAT?

On 14 November 1934 Arsenal provided seven of England's starting eleven for a friendly against world champions Italy, a record contribution which stands to this day. The game, since dubbed "The Battle of Highbury", took place at Arsenal Stadium and ended in a 3–2 victory for England. Frank Moss, George Male, Eddie Hapgood, Wilf Copping, Ray Bowden, Ted Drake and Cliff Bastin were the Arsenal players involved. Hapgood captained England for the first time while Drake and Male made their international debuts.

English Football League XI (1960–1990s)

1
John
LUKIC

2
Lee
DIXON

4
Tony
ADAMS

5
Steve
BOULD

3
Kenny
SANSOM

7
David
ROCASTLE

6
Michael
THOMAS

8
Alan
BALL

11
Brian
TALBOT

9
John
RADFORD

10
Charlie
GEORGE

DID YOU KNOW THAT?

Tony Adams, who bowed out as a player in 2002, rejoined the England set-up in 2013 when he was asked to coach the Under-19 team for a tie against Turkey. He made 66 appearances for England as a player, wearing the captain's armband for several of the ties.

DID YOU KNOW THAT?

Until 2011, Kenny Sansom held the record for the number of England caps won by a full-back, with 86 caps. His record was eclipsed by one-time Gunner, Ashley Cole.

English Premier League XI

DID YOU KNOW THAT?

David Platt's match-winning volley against Belgium in the 1990 World Cup finals was voted into the fans' top ten best England goals. Platt ultimately scored 27 goals in 67 England appearances, a fine tally for a midfielder.

DID YOU KNOW THAT?

Theo Walcott scored a hat-trick for England against Croatia in 2008, becoming the youngest player to score a hat-trick for the Three Lions.

Arsenal All-Ireland XI

1
Pat
JENNINGS

2
Pat
RICE

4
David
O'LEARY

5
Terry
MANCINI

3
Sammy
NELSON

7
Liam
BRADY

6
Joe
TONER

8
Joe
HAVERTY

11
Eddie
MCGOLDRICK

9
Niall
QUINN

10
Frank
STAPLETON

DID YOU KNOW THAT?
Niall Quinn is, at the time of writing, in the top 10 list of all-time appearance-makers and goal-scorers for the Republic of Ireland. He made 91 appearances and scored 21 goals between 1986 and 2002. Quinn turned out for his country at two World Cups, in 1990 and 2002.

DID YOU KNOW THAT?
David O'Leary scored the decisive penalty against Romania to put the Republic of Ireland into the quarter-finals at the 1990 World Cup.

Arsenal Scottish XI

1
Bob
WILSON

2
Archie
GRAY

4
Duncan
MCNICHOL

5
Frank
MCLINTOCK

3
Jimmy
JACKSON

7
George
GRAHAM

6
Roddy
MCEACHRANE

8
Jimmy
LOGIE

11
Alex
FORBES

9
Alex
JAMES

10
Charlie
NICHOLAS

DID YOU KNOW THAT?

Although Alex James made only eight appearances for Scotland, his brief international career included a 5-1 thrashing of England at Wembley in 1928, in which James scored twice.

DID YOU KNOW THAT?

Charlie Nicholas appeared for Scotland in the 1986 World Cup finals.

Arsenal European XI (up to 2002)

1
Jens
LEHMANN
(Germany)

2
Oleg
LUZHNIY
(Ukraine)

4
Remi
GARDE
(France)

5
Gilles
GRIMANDI
(France)

7
Marc
OVERMARS
(Holland)

6
Patrick
VIEIRA
(France)

8
Robert
PIRES
(France)

3
Anders
LIMPAR
(Sweden)

9
Dennis
BERGKAMP
(Holland)

10
Thierry
HENRY
(France)

11
Sylvain
WILTORD
(France)

DID YOU KNOW THAT?
Dennis Bergkamp scored a hat-trick for the Netherlands against Wales in 1996. He was his country's all-time leading goalscorer until Patrick Kluivert overtook him with his 38th goal in 2003.

DID YOU KNOW THAT?
Jens Lehmann set a national team record of not conceding a goal for 681 minutes during Germany's friendly against Switzerland in March 2008.

Arsenal European XI (post 2002)

1
Manuel
ALMUNIA
(Spain)

2
Bacary
SAGNA
(France)

4
William
GALLAS
(France)

5
Thomas
VERMAELEN
(Belgium)

3
Gael
CLICHY
(France)

7
Tomas
ROSICKY
(Czech Republic)

6
Cesc
FABREGAS
(Spain)

8
Freddie
LJUNGBERG
(Sweden)

11
Andrey
ARSHAVIN
(Russia)

9
Robin
VAN PERSIE
(Holland)

10
Lukas
PODOLSKI
(Germany)

DID YOU KNOW THAT?

Cesc Fabregas, whose senior international career began in 2006, represented Spain in four international tournaments between then and 2012, including Spain's winning campaigns at Euro 2008, the 2010 FIFA World Cup and Euro 2012.

DID YOU KNOW THAT?

Andrey Arshavin made an impassioned speech to FIFA before the voting which led to Russia winning the battle to host the 2018 World Cup.

Arsenal International Tournament XI

1
Jens
LEHMANN
(Germany)

2
LAUREN
(Cameroon)

4
Patrick
VIEIRA
(France)

5
Emmanuel
PETIT
(France)

3
John
JENSEN
(Denmark)

7
Cesc
FABREGAS
(Spain)

6
Santi
CAZORLA
(Spain)

8
Alan
BALL
(England)

11
GILBERTO
(Brazil)

9
Nwankwo
KANU
(Nigeria)

10
Thierry
HENRY
(France)

KEY

Jens Lehmann: World Cup semi-finalist (2006); **Lauren:** Olympic gold medallist (2000); **Emmanuel Petit:** World Cup Winner (1998); **John Jensen:** European Championship winner (1992); **Cesc Fabregas:** European Championship winner (2008, 2012), World Cup winner (2010); **Alan Ball:** World Cup winner (1966); **Patrick Vieira:** World Cup winner (1998), European Championship winner (2000); **Gilberto:** Copa America winner (2007); **Thierry Henry:** World Cup winner (1998), European Championship winner (2000); **Santi Cazorla:** European Championship winner (2008, 2012); **Nwankwo Kanu:** Olympic gold medallist (1996).

CHAPTER 6

Up for the Cup

With 10 FA Cup victories, a brace of League Cup triumphs and a pair of European final wins to its name, Arsenal can boast a rich heritage of knockout success. While league championships are generally considered the hardest honour to win, for the fans the sheer edge-of-the-seat drama of the cups is hard to beat. Between late winners, spectacular strikes and courageous comebacks, Arsenal have always provided drama aplenty in cup finals.

Beginning in Herbert Chapman's 1930s reign with the first FA Cup victory, this chapter chronicles the 14 cup finals Arsenal have won to date. From FA Cup wins over the likes of Huddersfield Town, Liverpool, Manchester United and Chelsea, to League Cup triumphs over Liverpool and Sheffield Wednesday, and triumphs in two European competitions.

Here you will find the important facts and figures for each final, together with a brief match report which between them will bring memories flooding back of those fabulous afternoons and evenings on which a Gunners captain proudly lifted a trophy.

FA Cup 1930

Three years after losing to Cardiff City in the FA Cup final, Herbert Chapman's men returned to Wembley in the same competition. The opposition would be the team Chapman had managed prior to Arsenal, Huddersfield Town. It had been a hard-fought route to the final for the Gunners, who had to prevail in tough encounters against Chelsea, Birmingham and Hull City. In the run-up to the final, Arsenal had enjoyed two balmy league results: beating Sheffield United 8–1 and drawing 6–6 at Leicester. On the big day, in front of a crowd of 92,298, the Gunners took the lead through Alex James after he exchanged passes with Cliff Bastin. Memorably, the *Graf Zeppelin*, Germany's giant airship, loomed sinisterly over the stadium during the first half, yet it was Huddersfield who laid siege to Charlie Preedy's goal. He somehow kept his sheet clean. With seven minutes left, Jack Lambert ran half the length of the field before doubling Arsenal's lead. When he had arrived at Highbury in the summer of 1925, Chapman had predicted it would take him five years to win silverware. His prediction had come true.

26 APRIL 1930, WEMBLEY STADIUM. ATT. 92,298

ARSENAL   2–0   HUDDERSFIELD TOWN

James, Lambert

Arsenal: Preedy, Parker, Hapgood, Baker, Seddon, John, Hulme, Jack, Lambert, James, Bastin.

DID YOU KNOW THAT?
In the commentary box that day was future Arsenal manager George Allison.

FA Cup 1936

A late goal from Ted Drake prevented plucky second division side Sheffield United from causing a cup upset in front of 93,384 spectators at Wembley Stadium. The Blades created and squandered a succession of chances, much to the relief of the Arsenal fans. Cliff Bastin endured a frustrating afternoon thanks to the attentions of Jackson and Hooper in the Blades' defence, until a 74th minute breakthrough. He tantalisingly drew his opponents before releasing the ball to Drake, who beat his man before letting fly with a terrific left-foot shot which powered into the top of the net. He had been a doubt prior to the match due to injury, yet Drake had been an energetic figure for most of the 90 minutes and, quite fittingly, won the tie. His celebration of the goal was short-lived. As his recent injury worries took their toll, he sunk onto his hands and knees, in terrible pain. Although he stayed on the field, he took no further part in the action. It had taken six years to come around, but the Gunners could put the FA Cup back in the trophy cabinet for a second time. Alex James was delighted to lift the famous trophy and the Gunners fans celebrated in style.

25 APRIL 1936, WEMBLEY STADIUM. ATT. 93,384

ARSENAL   1–0   SHEFFIELD UNITED

Drake

Arsenal: Wilson, Male, Hapgood, Crayston, Roberts, Copping, Hulme, Bowden, Drake, James, Bastin

DID YOU KNOW THAT?
The match receipts for the final amounted to just £24,857.

FA Cup 1950

The 1949–50 FA Cup campaign was kind to the Gunners. They were drawn at home in each round and even played their semi-final against Chelsea at White Hart Lane – thus, they didn't leave north London from start to glorious finish. Decked out in shirts of an "old gold" colour, the Gunners were in sparkling form against Liverpool. None shone brighter on the day than captain Joe Mercer. Liverpool had beaten Arsenal twice in the league that campaign, but at Wembley there was only one side in it once Tom Whittaker's team took the lead in the 17th minute. Jimmy Logie fed Reg Lewis whose shot beat Liverpool's Cyril Sidlow. Lewis was on target again on 62 minutes as he delightfully finished off a fine move that had been started by the imperious Mercer. With his 18th goal of the season, Lewis had drilled the ball into the bottom corner. Captain Mercer, recently crowned the Footballer of the Year, proudly led the triumphant Arsenal players up the Wembley steps to collect the FA Cup from King George VI. It was the third time the Club had won the famous trophy.

29 APRIL 1950, WEMBLEY STADIUM. ATT. 100,000
ARSENAL   2–0   LIVERPOOL
Lewis (2)
Arsenal: Swindin, Scott, Barnes, Forbes, D. Compton, Mercer, Cox, Logie, Goring, Lewis, L. Compton.

DID YOU KNOW THAT?
Mercer had been using the Liverpool training ground for his preparation for the match as his job was based in Merseyside.

European Fairs Cup 1970

Arsenal had gone 17 years without a trophy when they faced Anderlecht in the European Fairs Cup Final. After losing the first-leg 3–1, it appeared they would have to wait even longer for their next piece of silverware. It had all seemed so much brighter when they had seen off the mighty Ajax – featuring Johan Cruyff, Rudi Krol, Piet Keizer and Gerrit Muhren – in the semi-final. Following the first-leg defeat in Belgium, a rousing speech from captain Frank McLintock restored the team's confidence. In the second-leg at Highbury, Eddie Kelly and John Radford struck to level the aggregate scoreline. After Anderlecht hit the post to restore Arsenal jitters, Jon Sammels made it 3–0 on the night and 4–3 on aggregate. It had been a remarkable comeback from the Gunners! No team had ever come back from a two-goal deficit to win a two-legged European final, nor from a three-goal deficit at any point in a final. In achieving both feats, the Gunners completed a three-year residency for the trophy in England, as it had previously been won by Leeds United and Newcastle United.

28 APRIL 1970, HIGHBURY. ATT. 51,612
ARSENAL   3–0   ANDERLECHT
Kelly, Radford, Sammels   (SECOND LEG)
(Arsenal win 4–3 on aggregate)
Arsenal: Wilson, Storey, McNab, Kelly, McLintock, Simpson, Armstrong, Sammels, Radford, George, Graham.

DID YOU KNOW THAT?
Skipper Frank McLintock had been on the losing side in his four previous cup finals.

FA Cup 1971

Five days after clinching the league title at White Hart Lane, the Gunners were back in action at Wembley. The occasion? The small matter of an FA Cup final against Liverpool. Could Bertie Mee's team fulfil their dream of becoming the century's second winners of the domestic double? They could. Having needed a replay to overcome Stoke City in the semi-final, the players were under no illusions as to the scale of the challenge ahead. On a boiling hot day at Wembley, Ray Kennedy, George Graham and Charlie George wasted golden chances to give Arsenal the lead. The match went to extra-time, during which Liverpool's Steve Heighway broke the deadlock. Within minutes, Eddie Kelly, a second-half replacement for Peter Storey, poked the ball home to level the score. Then, the match and the season itself were gifted a glorious climax when Charlie George controlled a John Radford pass and volleyed home from 20 yards. He celebrated by lying on his back, with his arms outstretched. It became an iconic moment in the Club's history.

8 MAY 1971, WEMBLEY STADIUM. ATT. 100,000

ARSENAL   2–1   LIVERPOOL
Kelly, George   Heighway
(aet)

Arsenal: Wilson, Rice, McNab, Storey (Kelly), McLintock, Simpson, Armstrong, Graham, Radford, Kennedy, George.

DID YOU KNOW THAT?
When Liverpool's Chris Lawler collapsed due to cramp late in the game, two Arsenal players came to his assistance.

FA Cup 1979

Two goals ahead with just five minutes remaining, Arsenal looked set for a comfortable win in this tie. What happened next led to the match forever being remembered as "the five-minute final". United's Gordon McQueen and Sammy McIlroy scored in swift succession to cancel out Brian Talbot and Frank Stapleton's first half strikes for Arsenal. Terry Neill's side, and the Gunners fans, were shell-shocked. The drama was multiplied as Arsenal instantly regained the lead. Liam Brady took the ball deep into United's half and found Graham Rix who sent a dangerous cross into the box. Alan Sunderland arrived in the nick of time and stabbed the ball home. The Gunners, who had beaten Sheffield Wednesday, Notts County, Nottingham Forest, Southampton and Wolves en route to Wembley, gave the campaign the most dramatic of climaxes. Alan Sunderland celebrated his winner robustly – and why not? Meanwhile, Brian Talbot became only the second player to win an FA Cup medal with different clubs in successive seasons, having won in 1978 with Ipswich.

12 MAY 1979, WEMBLEY STADIUM. ATT. 100,000

ARSENAL   3-2   MANCHESTER UNITED

Talbot, Stapleton,   McQueen, McIlroy
Sunderland

Arsenal: Jennings, Rice, Nelson, Talbot, O'Leary, Young, Brady, Sunderland, Stapleton, Price (Walford), Rix.

DID YOU KNOW THAT?
The players wearing the numbers 1, 2, and 3 shirts for Arsenal that day – Pat Jennings, Pat Rice, and Sammy Nelson – had one thing in common: they came from Northern Ireland.

League Cup 1987

Back in 1987, a well-known statistic in English football was that Liverpool never lost a match in which Ian Rush scored. He had found the net in nearly 150 games for his club and the Reds won or drew all of those fixtures. So, when the prolific Welshman put the Anfield side ahead at Wembley, many neutrals joined the Liverpool faithful in writing the Gunners off. Charlie Nicholas had other ideas. The Scot equalised with a stabbed effort following a chaotic goalmouth scramble. He then netted the winner eight minutes from time when he met Perry Groves' cut-back with a shot that deflected past Bruce Grobbelaar. The Gunners celebrated wildly at the final whistle. They had won the first trophy of new manager George Graham's reign and overcome the then mighty Liverpool. Two years later they would accomplish another iconic – and more dramatic – victory over the Anfield giants, this time in the league.

5 APRIL 1987, WEMBLEY STADIUM. ATT. 96,000

ARSENAL   2–1   LIVERPOOL
Nicholas (2)   Rush

Arsenal: Lukic, Anderson, Sansom, Williams, O'Leary, Adams, Rocastle, Davis, Quinn (Groves), Nicholas, Hayes (Thomas).

DID YOU KNOW THAT?
The Gunners knocked out Spurs en route to Wembley, overcoming their great rivals in the semi-finals. Spurs hearts were also broken in the FA Cup that year, when they lost to Coventry in the final!

League Cup 1993

Steve Morrow was the unlikely hero of the day as the Gunners completed the first half of their cup double – yet his scoring of the winning goal would prove to be one memorable Morrow moment that day at Wembley. John Harkes opened the scoring for the Owls in the first-half, making history as the first American player to net in a Wembley final. However, Arsenal's Paul Merson was in magically influential form and he duly levelled the scoring. His first-time volley swerved agonisingly out of Chris Woods' reach. The perm-haired Gunner was also instrumental in the winner. His cross from the left was only partially dealt with by Carlton Palmer, allowing Morrow to race in and apply the deadly touch with a low shot. The Northern Irishman's post-match celebrations were cut short when he broke his arm after Tony Adams accidentally dropped him. Yet the Gunners had won the League Cup for a second time. In a season in which they would play Sheffield Wednesday on five occasions, they had won the first of three Wembley encounters between the two sides.

18 APRIL 1993, WEMBLEY STADIUM. ATT. 74,007
ARSENAL　2–1　SHEFFIELD WEDNESDAY
Merson, Morrow　　　　　Harkes

Arsenal: Seaman, O'Leary, Adams, Linighan, Winterburn, Parlour, Morrow, Davis, Merson, Wright, Campbell.

DID YOU KNOW THAT?
This was the first match in which players' shirts featured their name as well as number.

FA Cup 1993

The Gunners beat Yeovil, Leeds, Nottingham Forest and Ipswich en route to the 1993 semi-final. There, they faced local rivals Tottenham, who had beaten Arsenal at the same stage of the competition two years previously. Captain Tony Adams settled a tight match with a fine header, setting up a second final of the season with the Owls. The FA Cup final was therefore the fourth meeting of the season between the two sides, and it showed. A tight match ended all-square at 1–1, forcing the fixture to a replay and a fifth clash between the sides. There, Ian Wright slipped the ball past Chris Woods, only to see his strike cancelled out by a deflected shot from Chris Waddle to send the match into extra-time. With the tie seemingly headed to a penalty shoot-out, Andy Linighan rose to nod home a Merson corner. The defender, whose nose had been broken in the first-half, had heroically won the cup for Arsenal.

20 MAY 1993, WEMBLEY STADIUM. ATT. 62,267

ARSENAL   2–1   SHEFFIELD WEDNESDAY

Wright, Linighan   Waddle   (REPLAY)

(aet)

Arsenal: Seaman, Dixon, Winterburn, Linighan, Adams, Jensen, Davis, Smith, Merson, Campbell, Wright (O'Leary 81).

DID YOU KNOW THAT?
This game marked David O'Leary's final appearance for the Club. The Irishman served Arsenal for 20 years, putting in 722 appearances.

European Cup-Winners' Cup 1994

George Graham's men arrived in Copenhagen as firm underdogs for the showdown with Parma. Arsenal were missing talismanic striker Ian Wright and midfield anchor John Jensen through suspension, while Martin Keown was absent through injury. David Seaman needed pain-killing injections in a rib injury. The Italian side, meanwhile, boasted the likes of Tomas Brolin, Faustino Asprilla and Gianfranco Zola. Parma proved a great threat in the opening period of the match, coming close to taking the lead on several occasions. However, on 21 minutes a misjudged clearance from Minotti fell to lone striker Alan Smith on the edge of the area. The Englishman controlled the ball with his chest and fired a left-footed shot in off the post. As the team defended for their lives, the Gunners faithful cheered them on with ever louder renditions of the "One-nil to the Arsenal" chant. As the final whistle was blown, that proved to be the scoreline. Graham's team had done it. And no Arsenal smile was broader than that of match-winner Alan Smith.

4 MAY 1994, PARKEN STADIUM, COPENHAGEN. ATT. 33, 765
ARSENAL   1–0   PARMA
Smith
Arsenal: Seaman, Dixon, Winterburn, Davis, Bould, Adams, Campbell, Morrow, Smith, Merson (McGoldrick 86), Selley.

DID YOU KNOW THAT?
Manager George Graham described this as one of the two most satisfying matches of his reign. (The other was the 1989 league title clinching victory at Anfield.)

FA Cup 1998

A goal in either half of this final earned the Club its seventh FA Cup and the first "double" of Arsene Wenger's reign. The Gunners had won on the road four times during the FA Cup campaign, including a 4–3 penalty shoot-out win at West Ham in the sixth round. At Wembley, Kenny Dalglish's Newcastle United contributed to a tense opening quarter of the tie but in the 23rd minute, Arsenal got their noses in front. Emmanuel Petit found the speedy Marc Overmars and the Dutchman outpaced Alessandro Pistone before slotting the ball past Shay Given. Alan Shearer and Nikos Dabizas both made admirable attempts to level the score in the second half but Arsenal doubled their lead with 21 minutes left on the clock. Nicolas Anelka sprang onto Ray Parlour's pass and galloped into space before confidently sending the ball home. Overmars and man of the match Parlour almost added to the scoreline in the closing minutes.

16 MAY 1998, WEMBLEY STADIUM. ATT. 79,183
ARSENAL   2–0   NEWCASTLE UNITED
Overmars, Anelka

Arsenal: Seaman, Dixon, Adams, Keown, Winterburn, Parlour, Vieira, Petit, Overmars, Anelka, Wreh (Platt).

DID YOU KNOW THAT?
The Gunners squad featured six players who had taken part in the two FA Cup final matches of 1993: David Seaman, Lee Dixon, Nigel Winterburn, Tony Adams, Ian Wright and Ray Parlour.

FA Cup 2002

By now, the Gunners were in the opening stages of making the Millennium Stadium their second home. Wenger's team had not always left Wales triumphant, though. They went into this final with memories of their defeat at the hands of Liverpool in the previous campaign's final fresh in their heads. Having overcome Liverpool on their way to the 2002 final, Wenger's team were determined to avoid another Millennium Stadium heartbreak. David Seaman and a back-four marshalled by Tony Adams kept Chelsea at bay, before two cracking strikes from the Arsenal midfield settled the match. With 20 minutes left, Ray Parlour received the ball from Wiltord and volleyed home from 25 yards. The lead was doubled 10 minutes later when a gloriously in-form Freddie Ljungberg broke from the halfway line and curled a beauty past Carlo Cudicini. At the end of the match, there was an element of "changing of the guard" as Adams, playing in his last cup final, lifted the trophy with his successor-elect, Patrick Vieira. The Gunners had secured the first leg of the double – four days later they would secure the second.

4 MAY 2002, MILLENNIUM STADIUM, CARDIFF. ATT. 73,963

ARSENAL   2–0   CHELSEA
Parlour, Ljungberg

Arsenal: Seaman, Lauren, Campbell, Adams, Cole, Wiltord (Keown), Parlour, Vieira, Ljungberg, Bergkamp (Edu), Henry (Kanu).

DID YOU KNOW THAT?
Ljungberg's goal meant the Swede became the first man to score in successive Cup finals for 40 years.

FA Cup 2003

The Gunners retained the FA Cup for the first time thanks to a comfortable 1–0 victory over Southampton. Their passage to the final saw two relatively easy fixtures, against Oxford United and Farnborough Town, followed by tougher ties against Manchester United and Chelsea. Having overcome Sheffield United in the semi-final, they travelled to Cardiff to take on the Saints. Thierry Henry almost scored in the first 30 seconds, but was denied by Antti Niemi. Seven minutes before half-time, the Gunners were ahead. Henry played in Dennis Bergkamp who fed Freddie Ljungberg. When the Swede's shot was blocked, Frenchman Robert Pires buried the disappointment of missing the previous year's final by finding the back of the net from eight yards out. David Seaman was virtually untroubled until eight minutes from time when he heroically saved Brett Ormerod's soaring shot. Ashley Cole made a goal line clearance during injury time, confirming Arsenal's win.

17 MAY 2003, MILLENNIUM STADIUM, CARDIFF. ATT. 73,726
ARSENAL　　1–0　　SOUTHAMPTON
Pires

Arsenal: Seaman, Lauren, Keown, Luzhny, Cole, Pires, Parlour, Gilberto, Ljungberg, Henry, Bergkamp (Wiltord 77).

DID YOU KNOW THAT?
The match was the first FA Cup final to be played "indoors", with the Millennium Stadium roof closed because of inclement weather.

FA Cup 2005

On the road to their final FA Cup victory in Cardiff, Arsenal had taken on Stoke City, Wolverhampton Wanderers, Sheffield United, Bolton Wanderers and Blackburn Rovers. In the final, they were to face the mighty Manchester United. In truth, Arsenal were a little fortunate to win this, the first FA Cup final to be decided by a penalty shoot-out. Not a single Gunners fan was complaining as Patrick Vieira lifted the famous trophy after a tight encounter at Millennium Stadium. Wenger's team had failed to test Manchester United's Roy Carroll throughout the 90 minutes and subsequent extra-time. A wayward free-kick from Robin van Persie was the closest they came. United had several golden chances to score but wasted them all. Arsenal finished extra-time with 10 men, after Jose Antonio Reyes picked up a second yellow card. In the shoot-out, Jens Lehmann was the first to separate the sides when he pushed away Scholes' spot kick. That save proved decisive. In what would prove to be his last match for Arsenal, Patrick Vieira calmly slotted the ball into the top corner to win the trophy for the Gunners.

21 MAY 2005, MILLENNIUM STADIUM, CARDIFF. ATT. 71,876

ARSENAL   0–0   MANCHESTER UNITED

Arsenal win 5–4 on penalties after extra-time

Arsenal: Lehmann, Lauren, Toure, Senderos, Cole, Fabregas (Van Persie 86), Vieira, Gilberto, Pires (Edu 105), Bergkamp (Ljungberg 65), Reyes.

DID YOU KNOW THAT?

Rio Ferdinand had a "goal" ruled out on 21 minutes – it was struck off as he was offside.

CHAPTER 7

What the Gooners Said

Some people talk a good game, others play a good game. The very best of all are those who can both talk and play well. In the pages ahead you will find plenty of examples of this latter category, in this collection of memorable Arsenal quotes.

From serious and rousing sayings to cheeky soundbites and curious catchphrases, this is a compendium of Gunners-related pearls of wisdom that will keep all fans marvelling and chuckling accordingly. Some of the finest are from the French philosopher himself, Arsène Wenger. But the sayings here cross several decades and many eras.

Each page covers a different topic, from championship talk, goalscoring, the FA Cup and transfer talk. Then there is a page devoted to Mr Wenger, and another one which covers some of the more offbeat sayings that have been uttered during Arsenal's history. From short and sweet snapshots to more considered quotations, they are all here.

As you read through this selection you will probably also recall other fine sayings and quotes from Gunners folk down the years. Why not ask your friends for theirs, too. Between you, you could compile your own "squad" of Arsenal talk!

The Arsenal Way

1
"At some Clubs success is accidental. At Arsenal it is compulsory."

Arsène Wenger

2
"With us it is a case of goals and points. At times one is persuaded that nothing else matters."

Herbert Chapman

3
"Arsenal have got a certain class and dignity."

Ian Wright

4
"My wife gets a bit upset when I call Arsenal my 'first love'!"

Terry Burton

5
"Once an Arsenal man, always an Arsenal man."

Bob Wilson

Arsène Wenger

1

"Champions continue to go when normal human beings stop and that is what we want to show."

2

"We do not buy superstars, we make them."

3

"The star of the season was the squad."

4

"We all want to be the best and I believe I can be the best with Arsenal. I have a long-term vision for the Club."

5

"When you represent a club it's about values and qualities, not passports."

Happy Days

1
"Sometimes in life there is nothing better than being a Gooner."

Kevin Campbell

2
"I am really happy here and it is one of the best clubs I have ever seen. Everybody treats like you a king."

Cesc Fabregas

3
"I have not a single bad word to say for the Arsenal. It's a great club to play for."

Charlie Nicholas

4
"I was very lucky to play for Arsenal and win all those trophies."

Paul Merson

5
"I am Gooner."

Andrey Arshavin

Legends of the Shirt

1

"They talk about Bobby Moore and Dave Mackay as great captains, but for my money Frank McLintock is more inspiring than either of them."

Don Howe

2

"As far as I'm concerned, Tony Adams is like the Empire State Building."

Ian Wright

3

"If you selected a team of nice people, David Rocastle would be captain."

David O'Leary

4

"If you look at the whole package, with everything [Thierry] Henry has, I don't think you can find that anywhere else. You give him the ball in the right place and his acceleration will take him past any defender in the world."

Dennis Bergkamp

5

"I respect his fighting attitude. You could go to Sheffield or Bolton and know he will be ready to die to win the game."

Arsène Wenger on Patrick Vieira

The Invincibles

1

"I think we can go a whole season unbeaten."

Arsène Wenger, in 2002

2

"In 50 years time, people might still speak about it more than if you win the European Cup."

Wenger again, in 2004

3

"The Championship, and a place amongst history, goes to Arsenal!"

Martin Tyler, May 2004

4

"To remain unbeaten in a championship like the English championship now is really unbelievable. I want to win the Champions League but, really, this is more important."

Wenger puts the achievement in context

5

"This team is fantastic and we can play some great football. But we can dig in as well."

Sol Campbell

Champion Talk

1

"It was an amazing night. There were 40,000 locked outside and the coach had difficulty getting into the ground through the mass of heaving bodies."

Frank McLintock on the 1971 title

2

"We got a standing ovation from the Kop, who had stayed there [after the final whistle] because I think they appreciated the way we'd gone about the game."

Perry Groves on the climax of the 1988–89 championship

3

"It must have been good for the fans to see us repeat what happened in 1971 when we also won the title at Tottenham."

Arsène Wenger on winning the league at White Hart Lane in 2004

4

"We were blessed with a backbone of men with character who demanded excellence from others."

Don Howe, 1971

5

"I am going to make this the greatest Club in the world."

Herbert Chapman foreshadows his title triumphs

Tottenham Talk

1

"I didn't score as many as I hoped, but it was nice that I always seemed to score against Tottenham."

Charlie Nicholas

2

"Spurs are a great Club, they showed that they can play really good football, but are they really better than Arsenal? I don't think so."

Wojciech Szczesny

3

"I tried to watch the Tottenham match on television in my hotel yesterday, but I fell asleep."

Arsène Wenger, 1996

4

"I went to Barcelona with Monaco and there were 120,000 people there. Yet it was almost quiet compared with our game against Spurs at Highbury."

Arsene Wenger, 1997

5

"Arsenal have got as much chance of being handed the title by Spurs as I have of being given the crown jewels."

Spurs captain Alan Mullery before the last match of the 1971 season

Thrill of the FA Cup

1

"I just stood up and raised my hands to the heavens. I was saying a prayer of thanks."

Terry Neill on his reaction to Alan Sunderland's last-minute winner against Manchester United in the 1979 FA Cup final

2

"A broken nose is nothing. I tried to get one throughout my playing career because it adds character to your face."

George Graham on the injury picked-up by match-winner Andy Linighan in the 1993 FA Cup final replay.

3

"There wasn't a lot of support, so I thought 'Why not?' and the next thing I knew it was in the back of the net."

Ray Parlour on his wonder volley in the 2002 FA Cup final

4

"People say why did I lie on the floor after the goal, they said I was tired. But I think I was a lot cleverer than people thought."

Charlie George on his famous, and time-wasting, celebration after scoring the winner in the 1971 FA Cup final.

5

"I am going to ask you for the sake of this football club to put your family second for the next month. You have the chance to put your names in the record books for all time."

Bertie Mee, after Arsenal qualified for the 1971 FA Cup final

Scoring, Scoring, Arsenal

1

*"He convinced himself that he could not score goals
but I thought let's have a go and start you from the
centre. We worked on him with finishing and he
became a tremendous goalscorer."*

Arsène Wenger on Thierry Henry

2

*"5–2 is too cavalier. I would have preferred
2–0 or 3–0."*

George Graham, following a home victory vs. Sheffield United, 1991

3

*"It is not so enjoyable to score goals if the team does
not win."*

Freddie Ljungberg

4

*"He is definitely the best goalscorer I have played with.
In terms of snapping up half chances there was nobody
better than Ian [Wright]."*

Alan Smith

5

*"He had a trait few of us are blessed with
– an ice-cold nerve."*

Tom Whittaker on then-record goalscorer Cliff Bastin

Transfer Talk

1

"We nearly didn't sign him because the letters did not fit on his shirt."

David Dein on Giovanni van Bronckhorst

2

"Other Clubs never came into my thoughts once I knew Arsenal wanted to sign me."

Dennis Bergkamp

3

"A player's value should be judged on his ability to fit in with the other members of the team. The best player who ever kicked a ball would be small use if he were as one apart. This is the danger of every transfer."

Herbert Chapman

4

"He was upset at the rumours he was not fit and that he could never play to his true ability again. That was a good sign for me, a hurt player. He had something to prove."

Arsène Wenger on Marc Overmars

5

"You're not even taking a risk."

Bob Wilson's response to George Graham when the manager asked him his advice on the proposed purchase of David Seaman

CHAPTER 8

Sing Your Hearts Out For The Lads

Throughout the Club's history one thing has remained the same – the hearty efforts of Gunners supporters to cheer on the boys in red and white. The songs and chants have evolved over the years as Arsenal fans have aimed to sing their way to becoming the team's "twelfth man", urging the team on to another cherished victory.

In the coming pages you will find a selection of the most memorable songs and chants that have been heard at Arsenal matches. Some of them are timeless classics, others are songs whose lyrics apply to and evoke a particular era in the evolution of London's finest club.

There is, arguably, no greater way for the fans to show their support for the Gunners than by cheering them on from the stands. So this chapter allows you to recall some classic songs from times past, and to join in with the current ones and become part of football's finest red-and-white choir.

As Arsène Wenger once told the Arsenal faithful: "You are every bit as important as every other part of the operation and I thank you for your vocal and warm support." The Frenchman added: "You are a key part of every victory we enjoy."

Good Old Arsenal

Good old Arsenal,
We're proud to say that name.
And while we sing this song,
We'll win the game.

You Are My Arsenal

You are my Arsenal! My only Arsenal!
You make me happy! When skies are grey!
You'll never know just, how much I love you!
So please don't take my Arsenal away!
Na na na na na – ooh
Na na na na na – ooh

By Far The Greatest Team

And it's Arsenal... (clap, clap, clap)
Arsenal FC...
We're by far the greatest team,
The world has ever seen.

DID YOU KNOW THAT?
The Club released *Good Old Arsenal* as their FA Cup final
song in 1971. The song, whose lyrics were written by Jimmy
Hill, peaked at No.16 in the British charts.

She Wore A Yellow Ribbon

She wore,
She wore,
She wore a yellow ribbon,
She wore a yellow ribbon in the merry month of May,
And when,
I asked,
Oh why she wore that ribbon,
She said it's for the Arsenal and we're going to Wembley,
Wembley,
Wembley,
We're the famous Arsenal and we're going Wembley.

We Won The League On Merseyside

We won the league! (We won the league!)
On Merseyside! (On Merseyside!)
We won the league on Merseyside...
We won the league, on the Mersey...
We won the league on Merseyside!

We All Follow The Arsenal

We all follow the Arsenal,
Over land and sea, (and Tottenham!)
We all follow the Arsenal,
Onto victory!

B'Jesus Said Paddy

B'Jesus said Paddy I sang it so well,
I think I'll get up and I'll sing it again, so Paddy got up
and he sang it again, Over and Over and Over again.

A Perry Groves World

Number 1 is Perry Groves!
Number 2 is Perry Groves!
Number 3 is Perry Groves!
Number 4 is Perry Groves!
Number 5 is Perry Groves!
Number 6 is Perry Groves!
Number 7 is Perry Groves!
Number 8 is Perry Groves!
Number 9 is Perry Groves!
Number 10 is Perry Groves!
Number 11 is Perry Groves!
Number 12 is Perry Groves!
(all together now!)
We all live in a Perry Groves world
A Perry Groves world
A Perry Groves world

This song, set to the tune of *Yellow Submarine* by The Beatles,
is an inventive and affectionate tribute to Arsenal's cult hero
of the 1980s, Perry Groves. The ginger winger even named his
memoir, *We All Live In A Perry Groves World*, after the ditty.

One-Nil To The Arsenal

One-nil to the Arsenal,
One-nil to the Arsenal,
One-nil to the Arsenal,
One-nil to the Arsenal,
One-nil to the Arsenal!

This song, set to the tune of the Village People hit *Go West*, became the Gunners fans' anthem during the successful march to the 1994 European Cup-Winners' Cup final. The scoreline in the final was, appropriately, 1–0 to the Arsenal. Ian Wright later recorded a version of the song with himself on vocals, which was featured on a Club end-of-season video.

One Team in London

One team in London!
There's only one team in London!
One team in London!
There's only one team in London!

Ooh to be a Gooner

Ooh to,
Ooh to be,
Ooh to be a – Gooner!

Wenger's Magic Hat

Arsène Wenger's Magic!
He wears a magic hat.
And when he saw the Premier League,
He said I'm having that!

We Love You Arsenal

We love you Arsenal, we do!
We love you Arsenal, we do!
We love you Arsenal! we do!
Ohhh Arsenal we love you!

Super Jack

Super, Super Jack!
Super, Super Jack!
Super Jacky Wilshere!

Are You Tottenham in Disguise?

Are you Tottenham,
Are you Tottenham,
Are you Tottenham in disguise?
Are you Tottenham in disguise?

Who's That Team?

Who's that team they call the Arsenal,
Who's that team we all adore,
We're the boys in red and white and we fight with all our might,
And we're out to show the world the way to score.

Thierry The King

Thierry Henry came to us from Turin
Not sure about playing up front or the wing
Then Arsène had a word and he said he was keen,
To make him the best striker we've ever seen...
Thierry, Thierry, Thierry, Thierry
Born is the King of Highbury!

The Arsenal Anthem

And did those boots of Arsenal's team
Walk upon Highbury's turf so green?
And did they play with great esteem
The best football we've ever seen?
And with a cannon on our chest
We play with heart, and mind, and zest
And we are proud to be Arsenal

CHAPTER 9

Arsenal Supporters' Quiz

In this chapter you can put your Arsenal fandom to the test. Here are 10 quizzes, each containing 20 questions, on every aspect of Arsenal Football Club. They are a perfect way to pass the time on the way to your next Gunners match, as a series of half-time teasers, or perhaps as an impromptu pub quiz with your fellow Gooners.

The first seven rounds each cover a particular era in the Club's history, including the Early Years of Arsenal, Herbert Chapman's reign, and the Wenger era. The other three are devoted to great European nights, the Club's various stadiums and the Invincibles' glorious 49-match unbeaten run. As well as testing your memory to the limits, the quizzes will bring back fond memories of the Club's illustrious history.

Do you know your Ted Drake from your Thierry Henry, your Manor Ground from your Malcolm Macdonald? And how knowledgeable are you on the contents of Arsenal's trophy cabinet? Fancy yourself as more of a final-winning fan than a mid-table part-timer? Then put yourself to the test here – and good luck to you.

Quiz 1: The Early Years

1   What was the first name of the Club?
2   And what did they quickly change the name to?
3   Who were the Club's first opponents: Eastern Wanderers or Euston Wanderers?
4   In which year did the Club play that match?
5   Arrivals from which Midlands team prompted the Club to adopt a red shirt?
6   What was the name of the Club's first boss, whose title was "Secretary Manager"?
7   In which year did the Club turn professional?
8   True or false: one of the Club's early homes was the Invicta Ground.
9   In which year did the Club first gain promotion to Division One?
10 Who was Arsenal's manager in the years following the end of the First World War?
11 Which team did Arsenal beat 12–0 in March 1900?
12 The Club's original socks were white and which other colour?
13 The Club's first crest was based on the coat of arms of which borough?
14 What was the name of the area the Club hired on Plumstead Marshes?
15 By how many teams was the First Division extended following the First World War, benefiting Arsenal?
16 Name Arsenal's second manager.
17 How many seasons was third manager, George Elcoat, in charge for?
18 Name the Scot who was appointed boss in 1904.
19 Which team did Sam Hollis move to after Arsenal?
20 Name the opponents for Arsenal's final match at the Manor Ground.

Quiz 2: The Herbert Chapman Era

1 With which club did Chapman win the FA Cup and two Division One titles prior to joining the Gunners?

2 In his first season as Arsenal manager, Chapman guided the Club to its highest league position to date. What position was it?

3 He guided the Club to its first FA Cup final. Who were the opponents?

4 In which year did Arsenal win its first FA Cup, beating Chapman's old team Huddersfield Town?

5 How many points did the Gunners amass in their first league championship campaign of 1930–31: 66 or 45?

6 Name the striker who, having made his name during Chapman's reign, went on to score 178 goals in 395 games?

7 Which trophy did the Gunners win in 1931–32?

8 Who took over the Club after Chapman's tragic death in 1934?

9 And how many successive league titles did he win?

10 How many goals did Ted Drake score in the 1934–35 season?

11 Which player's kneecap is stored at Middlesex County Cricket Club?

12 True or false: in the 1937–38 season champions Arsenal scored less goals than relegated Manchester City.

13 Arsenal won the title in 1935. But which side finished bottom of the league that year?

14 True or false: The Gunners scored 127 league goals in the 1930–31 season?

15 Which commercial deal, later held by David Beckham, did Denis Compton famously secure?

16 In which English county was Herbert Chapman born?

17 True or false: Herbert Chapman had previously managed Leeds United.

18 How many Arsenal players did England field against world champions Italy on 14 November 1934?

19 Which team did the Gunners thrash 9–1 in the 1930–31 season?

20 In which year did the East Stand officially open?

Quiz 3: The 1940s and '50s

1 True or false: Stanley Matthews appeared for the Club as a "guest player" during the Second World War?
2 In which year was Highbury bombed?
3 Who scored four times as the Gunners beat Charlton 7–1 in the League South Cup final?
4 And who were the opponents when a goal from the same player won the 1950 FA Cup final?
5 Which manager guided the Gunners to the 1947–48 league championship?
6 Name the Gunners striker who won the Golden Boot, scoring 33 goals in that campaign?
7 Which player succeeded Leslie Compton as captain when the latter concentrated on cricketing duties with Middlesex?
8 What mistake did the Queen make at the end of the 1950 FA Cup final?
9 What was the wafer-thin goal average margin by which Arsenal pipped Preston to the 1952–53 championship?
10 What is the relevance of the home tie against Manchester United on 1 February 1958?
11 What was the scoreline when Arsenal beat Blackpool in the 1953 Charity Shield: 1–0 or 3–1?
12 When the Gunners won the 1948 championship, how many titles in total had they won?
13 Who managed the Club between 1956 and 1958?
14 Who were the opponents for the first floodlit match at Highbury?
15 Which career did Gunner Gordon Nutt enter after leaving Arsenal?
16 Name one of the other sports in which Dr Kevin O'Flanagan had competed?
17 How many Arsenal players died in the Second World War?
18 True or false: Arsenal won the 1952 FA Cup.
19 In which decade did Arsenal first wear an "away shirt"?
20 Name the year Arsène Wenger was born in.

The 1960s and '70s

1 Which job at the Club had Bertie Mee held prior to becoming manager?

2 Name the team the Gunners beat in the 1970 Fairs Cup final.

3 In which two successive years did Arsenal finish runners-up in the League Cup final?

4 Who scored the winner in Arsenal's 1971 FA Cup final against Liverpool?

5 True or false: the Gunners won the 1970–71 league title at Anfield.

6 In which year, famous in English football, did Arsenal win the Youth Cup?

7 Which team beat Arsenal in the 1972 FA Cup final?

8 Name the former Spurs goalkeeper signed by Terry Neill?

9 How many successive FA Cup finals did Arsenal reach starting in 1978?

10 And what was the score when they beat Manchester United at Wembley in 1979?

11 How many times were Arsenal drawn at home during the victorious 1970–71 FA Cup campaign?

12 Name the Scot who had appeared on the losing side in four cup finals before winning the FA Cup in 1971.

13 Which third trophy did Arsenal win in the 1970–71 "double" year?

14 An Arsenal match in August 1964 was the first to be screened on the new BBC show *Match of the Day*. Name the opponents.

15 Which young Gunner was described as "a world star of the future" by Johan Cruyff following a Fairs Cup tie with Ajax?

16 How many League Cup finals did Arsenal reach in the 1960s?

17 In what league position did the Club finish in 1969?

18 Which Second Division side knocked Arsenal out of the 1960 FA Cup?

19 What was the scoreline when the Gunners beat Spurs on 23 December 1978?

20 Who nodded the goal that secured Arsenal the 1971 league title?

Quiz 5: The George Graham Era

1 Who did Graham succeed as manager?
2 Name two other London sides managed by Graham.
3 Who did the Gunners beat in the 1987 League Cup final?
4 Michael Thomas scored the famous winner at Anfield in May 1989, but who scored Arsenal's other goal that night?
5 How many matches did Arsenal lose on their way to the 1990–91 league title?
6 Which team did Arsenal beat in the FA Cup and League Cup finals of 1993?
7 Which side did goal machine Ian Wright join the Club from?
8 In which city did the Gunners win the 1994 European Cup-Winners' Cup final?
9 Name George Graham's immediate successor.
10 Which former Bolton Wanderers boss bought Dennis Bergkamp to the Club in 1995?
11 As well as Graham, how many other "Georges" have managed the Club?
12 Alan Smith received only one booking in his career. Against which team?
13 Which shirt number did Dennis Bergkamp wear?
14 What was the title of Graham's autobiography?
15 How many goals did Eddie McGoldrick score for Arsenal?
16 True or false: Andy Cole never appeared in the Arsenal first team?
17 Name Graham's final purchase as Arsenal boss.
18 And in which year had Graham been appointed Arsenal manager?
19 True or false: Graham was a previous Arsenal player.
20 Name the Swedish winger who terrorised defences for Arsenal in the 1990–91 title campaign.

Quiz 6: The Arsène Wenger Era (Part 1)

1 From which club did Wenger arrive: Grampus Eight or Cowdenbeath?
2 Name the future Club captain who was one of the Frenchman's first purchases.
3 Which side did the Gunners beat in the 1998 FA Cup final to secure the "double"?
4 Ian Wright beat which player's all-time goalscoring record in 1997?
5 Tony Adams and which other England captain featured in the 1997–98 side?
6 Name the Dutch winger who terrorised defences for Wenger's side.
7 Which side did Arsenal face over two epic matches in the 1999 FA Cup semi-final?
8 Who did the team face in the 2000 UEFA Cup final?
9 In which year did Thierry Henry join the Gunners?
10 How many managers from outside the UK had Arsenal appointed prior to Wenger?
11 Which football magazine named Wenger one of "Six Men Who Changed Football" in 2006?
12 Which instrument did captain Tony Adams learn in the late 1990s?
13 Which midfielder injured himself while celebrating a goal against Manchester United in 1997?
14 Name the team that Dennis Bergkamp, Thierry Henry and Marc Overmars all broke their Gunners scoring duck against.
15 Which player became the first Austrian to play in the Premiership?
16 Nigel Winterburn and which other player did Wenger describe as "like two good bottles of French wine – the older they get, the better they are"?
17 True or false: Wenger was the second manager to join the Club from a Japanese side.
18 At Monaco Wenger had won the French Cup and which other major honour?
19 Name the midfielder Wenger managed at both Monaco and Arsenal.
20 Which position had Wenger held at AS Cannes?

Quiz 7: The Arsène Wenger Era (Part 2)

1   Which side finished runners-up to Arsenal in the 2002 league table?
2   At which stadium did the Gunners secure the title?
3   And which London rivals did Arsenal beat in the FA Cup final in the same season?
4   Ray Parlour and which other player scored in the final?
5   How many matches did it take Thierry Henry to become the Club's top scorer with 186 goals: 303 games or 403 games?
6   Name the Nigerian striker who scored a match-winning hat-trick against Chelsea in 1999.
7   Which team did the Gunners beat 7–0 in May 2005?
8   Name the French striker who returned to the Club for a second spell in 2012.
9   Which FA Cup feat did the Gunners achieve in May 2003?
10 Name the city Wenger was born in.
11 In which two successive seasons did Arsenal top the Barclays Premiership Fair Play League?
12 Other than Wenger, how many Gunners managers have won the FA Cup more than once?
13 Name the midfielder who scored in both the 2001 and 2002 FA Cup finals.
14 Which local honour did Wenger receive in 2004?
15 How many months after joining Arsenal did Theo Walcott make his debut?
16 In which years was Wenger named Coach of the Year at the BBC Sports Personality awards?
17 Which team did the Gunners beat on penalties in the 2005 FA Cup final?
18 Which player scored his 100th Arsenal goal in a tie against Oxford United in 2003?
19 Name the goalkeeper who kept a clean sheet for 853 minutes of Champions League football in 2005 and 2006.
20 Which shirt number did William Gallas wear?

Quiz 8: European Glory Nights

1   Which Spanish side were beaten by a Thierry Henry wonder goal in the 2005–06 season?
2   Which former Gunners star was part of the Juventus team beaten by Arsenal in 2006?
3   Who scored the winner as Arsenal beat Parma in the 1994 European Cup-Winners' Cup final?
4   Name the team Arsenal beat 6–1 in the 1991 European Cup.
5   Juventus' Roberto Bettega scored an own goal at Highbury to level the score in the semi-final of which competition?
6   True or false: the Gunners beat AC Milan in the semi-final of the 1995 European Cup-Winners' Cup.
7   And who were Arsenal's semi-final opponents the previous year?
8   Name the French opponents Arsenal faced in their first ever UEFA Champions League tie in 1998.
9   How old was John Lukic when he appeared against Lazio in 2000?
10 And how old was Jack Wilshere when he took to the field against Dynamo Kyiv 2008?
11 Which side did Edu and Robert Pires help the Gunners beat 3–2, the Club's first Champions League victory in Spain?
12 Name the Italian giants Arsenal beat 5–1 in November 2003, their first home loss to an English side since the 1960s.
13 Name the Gunner who struck the equaliser when Arsenal drew 1–1 with Barcelona at the Nou Camp in 1999.
14 Which team did the Gunners face in the 2006 Champions League semi-final?
15 Which side did Arsenal beat 10–0 on aggregate during the 1993–94 European Cup-Winners' Cup campaign?
16 In which year did Arsenal play their first home European tie?
17 Which team did Arsenal beat 7–0 in the 2007 Champions League?
18 How many Champions League ties did Thierry Henry feature in for the Club: 60 or 70?
19 And who were the European opponents when Henry became the Club's number one goalscorer?
20 Whose semi-final penalty save booked the Gunners their place in the 2006 Champions League final?

Quiz 9: Stadium Stumpers

1. True or false: the stadium known as "Highbury" was not actually called Highbury.
2. Name the 1940s movie filmed at the stadium.
3. What was Arsenal tube station originally named?
4. Name the ground the Gunners played in prior to moving to Highbury.
5. What was the original name for Highbury's North Bank?
6. In which year did the Gunners move to Emirates Stadium?
7. Who were the opponents for the first competitive match at the Emirates?
8. And which Club legend's testimonial was the first friendly at the Club's new home?
9. Name the opponents for Arsenal's first home match at the Manor Ground.
10. Which year did Arsenal move to the Invicta Ground?
11. Which member of the Royal Family opened Emirates Stadium on 26 October 2006?
12. Which Brazilian scored the new stadium's first goal in August 2006?
13. True or false: Carlos Vela netted the stadium's first hat-trick.
14. The Emirates has hosted many rock concerts, but who performed the first?
15. The first eight Premier League ties at the Emirates ended either 3–0 or which other scoreline?
16. What role did Archibald Leitch play in the history of Highbury?
17. Against which team did Thierry Henry score a hat-trick in Highbury's final match?
18. Which artistic style was the East Stand designed in?
19. In which district of London was the Manor Ground situated?
20. How many banks of terracing were there in the original Highbury design?

Quiz 10: The 49ers

1 In which month of 2003 did Arsenal's historic 49-match unbeaten run commence?

2 Which goalkeeper appeared in 47 of the 49 matches?

3 Name the Frenchman who scored a crucial goal against Liverpool in April 2004, despite carrying a back injury.

4 Even once the unbeaten run ended in October 2004, the Gunners remained unbeaten at home until...?

5 Which Brazilian legend said the "Invincibles" team played "samba football"?

6 How many of the 49 matches did the Gunners draw?

7 And how many goals did they score?

8 Who were the opponents as the Gunners sealed an entire league season unbeaten in May 2004?

9 Which Midlands side did Arsenal beat in the final tie of the 49-match run?

10 What was the score when Arsenal beat Southampton in the first tie of the run?

11 How many goalless draws where there in the run?

12 How many points did Arsenal amass during the run?

13 How many players appeared during the run: 23 or 33?

14 And how many different Gunners scored: 15 or 8?

15 How many goals did Robert Pires net?

16 Which Manchester United striker hit the bar with a penalty against Arsenal at Old Trafford?

17 Which defender bowed out of the Club with a friendly against an England line-up in May 2004?

18 Name one of the players who scored for Arsenal in the 49th match of the unbeaten run.

19 When Arsenal beat Liverpool 4–2 in April 2004, what had the half-time scoreline been?

20 How many goals did the Gunners average per game during the unbeaten run?

Answers

Quiz 1: The Early Years

1 Dial Square. **2** Royal Arsenal. **3** Eastern Wanderers. **4** 1886. **5** Nottingham Forest. **6** Sam Hollis. **7** 1891. **8** True. **9** 1903. **10** Leslie Knighton. **11** Loughborough. **12** Blue. **13** Woolwich. **14** Sportsman Ground. **15** Two. **16** Thomas Brown Mitchell. **17** One. **18** Phil Kelso. **19** Bristol City. **20** Middlesbrough.

Quiz 2: The Herbert Chapman Era

1 Huddersfield Town. **2** Second place in Division One. **3** Cardiff City. **4** 1930. **5** 66. **6** Cliff Bastin. **7** Charity Shield. **8** George Allison. **9** Two. **10** 42. **11** Denis Compton. **12** True. **13** Tottenham Hotspur. **14** True. **15** Brylcreem Boy. **16** Yorkshire. **17** False – it was Leeds City. **18** Seven. **19** Grimsby Town. **20** 1936.

Quiz 3: The 1940s and '50s

1 True. **2** 1941. **3** Reg Lewis. **4** Liverpool. **5** Tom Whittaker. **6** Ronnie Rooke. **7** Joe Mercer. **8** She accidentally handed Joe Mercer a loser's medal. **9** By 0.099 of a goal. **10** It was the last game the Busby Babes played before the Munich disaster. **11** 3–1. **12** Six. **13** Jack Crayston. **14** Hapoel Tel Aviv. **15** The movie industry – he became a film director. **16** Rugby or athletics. **17** Nine. **18** False – they finished runners-up. **19** The 1950s. **20** 1949.

Quiz 4: The 1960s and '70s

1 Physiotherapist. **2** Anderlecht. **3** 1968 and 1996. **4** Charlie George. **5** False – it was won at White Hart Lane. **6** 1966. **7** Leeds United. **8** Pat Jennings. **9** Three. **10** 3–2. **11** Zero. **12** Frank McLintock. **13** The FA Youth Cup. **14** Liverpool. **15** Charlie George. **16** Two. **17** Fourth. **18** Rotherham. **19** 5–0 to Arsenal. **20** Ray Kennedy.

Quiz 5: The George Graham Era

1 Don Howe. **2** Millwall and Spurs. **3** Liverpool. **4** Alan Smith. **5** One. **6** Sheffield Wednesday. **7** Crystal Palace. **8** Copenhagen. **9** Stewart Houston. **10** Bruce Rioch. **11** Four – George Elcoat, George Morrell, George Allison and George Swindin. **12** Sheffield Wednesday. **13** Number 10. **14** *The Glory and the Grief*. **15** One. **16** False – he made a total of six minutes of first team action against Sheffield United in December 1990. **17** Glenn Helder.

18 1986. **19** True. **20** Anders Limpar.

Quiz 6: The Arsène Wenger Era (Part 1)

1 Grampus Eight. **2** Patrick Vieira. **3** Newcastle United. **4** Cliff Bastin. **5** David Platt. **6** Marc Overmars. **7** Manchester United. **8** Galatasaray. **9** 1999. **10** None. **11** *FourFourTwo*. **12** Piano. **13** Patrick Vieira. **14** Southampton. **15** Alex Manninger. **16** Steve Bould. **17** False – he was the first. **18** The French championship. **19** Emmanuel Petit. **20** Assistant Manager.

Quiz 7: The Arsène Wenger Era (Part 2)

1 Liverpool. **2** Old Trafford. **3** Chelsea. **4** Freddie Ljungberg. **5** 303. **6** Nwankwo Kanu. **7** Everton. **8** Thierry Henry. **9** They retained the trophy for the first time in the Club's history. **10** Strasbourg. **11** 2003–04 and 2004–05. **12** None. **13** Freddie Ljungberg. **14** He was awarded the Freedom of the Borough of Islington. **15** Seven. **16** 2002 and 2004. **17** Manchester United. **18** Dennis Bergkamp. **19** Jens Lehmann. **20** 10.

Quiz 8: European Glory Nights

1 Real Madrid. **2** Patrick Vieira. **3** Alan Smith. **4** Austria Vienna. **5** European Cup-Winners' Cup. **6** False – it was Sampdoria. **7** Paris St Germain. **8** RC Lens. **9** 39. **10** 16. **11** Celta Vigo. **12** Inter Milan. **13** Nwankwo Kanu. **14** Villarreal. **15** Standard Liege. **16** 1963. **17** Slavia Prague. **18** 70. **19** Sparta Prague. **20** Jens Lehmann.

Quiz 9: Stadium Stumpers

1 True – it was officially called Arsenal Stadium. **2** *The Arsenal Stadium Mystery*. **3** Gillespie Road. **4** The Manor Ground. **5** The Laundry End. **6** 2006. **7** Aston Villa. **8** Dennis Bergkamp. **9** Newcastle United. **10** 1890. **11** Prince Philip. **12** Gilberto. **13** False – it was Emmanuel Adebayor (though Vela did score the stadium's second hat-trick). **14** Bruce Springsteen. **15** 1–1. **16** He designed the stadium. **17** Wigan Athletic. **18** Art Deco. **19** Plumstead. **20** Three.

Quiz 10: The 49ers

1 May. **2** Jens Lehmann. **3** Thierry Henry. **4** 1 February 2005. **5** Roberto Carlos. **6** 13. **7** 112. **8** Leicester City. **9** Aston Villa. **10** 6–1 to Arsenal. **11** Four. **12** 121. **13** 33. **14** 15. **15** 23. **16** Ruud van Nistelrooy. **17** Martin Keown. **18** Thierry Henry, Cesc Fabregas or Jose Antonio Reyes. **19** 2–1 to Liverpool. **20** 2.3.

Picture Quiz Answers

PICTURE QUIZ 1: Gatherings of the Arsenal faithful
A Manor Ground, Plumstead. **B** Highbury. **C** Wembley Stadium.
D Emirates.

PICTURE QUIZ 2: Simply Hair-Raising
A Freddie Ljungberg. **B** Cesc Fabregas. **C** Gervinho.
D Marouane Chamakh.

PICTURE QUIZ 3: Celebrate Good Times
A Charlie George, 1971 FA Cup Final. **B** Alan Sunderland, 1979 FA
Cup Final. **C** Michael Thomas, 1989 League Championship decider.
D Thierry Henry, 10 January 2012 comeback goal.

PICTURE QUIZ 4: The Road to Rio
A Thomas Vermaelen (Belgium). **B** Lukas Podolski (Germany). **C** Theo
Walcott (England). **D** Wojciech Szczesny (Poland).

PICTURE QUIZ 5: Remind You of Anybody?
A Rodders (Tony Adams). **B** Shergar (Nicolas Anelka). **C** Chippy
(Liam Brady) **D** The Flying Dutchman (Dennis Bergkamp).

PICTURE QUIZ 6: Meet the Gaffer
A George Graham. **B** Don Howe. **C** George Swindin. **D** Terry Neill.

PICTURE QUIZ 7: They Shall Not Pass
A David Seaman (Englishman). **B** Bob Wilson (Scotsman). **C** Pat
Jennings (Irishman). **D** Jack Kelsey (Welshman).

PICTURE QUIZ 8: New Kid on the Block
A Peter Marinello (Hibernian). **B** Malcolm Macdonald (Newcastle
United). **C** Charlie Nicholas (Celtic). **D** Andrey Arshavin (Zenit St
Petersburg).